DIRECT CONNECTION'S

Guide to

FUNDRAISING ON THE INTERNET

Acknowledgements

The author wishes to thank Penny Yates-Mercer of City University, Kim Worts of Aurelian Publishing Ltd, Computing Services Department at City University for allowing UK Fundraising to remain on their server, all those who have offered suggestions and advice for both UK Fundraising and this book, the fundraising discussion list-owners and creators, and the many fundraisers who share their experience and skills freely on those lists every day.

This book is dedicated to Wendy Clifton-Sprigg

The information in this book is believed to be correct at the time of going to press, but must not be treated as a substitute for detailed advice in individual situations. It is published without responsibility on the part of Aurelian Information Ltd or Howard Lake, whether arising from any negligence, misrepresentation or otherwise for loss occasioned to any person or organisation acting or refraining from acting as a result of any information contained herein.

Printed in England by Powage Press, Aspley Guise, Milton Keynes MK17 8HF

DIRECT CONNECTION'S

Guide to

FUNDRAISING ON THE INTERNET

Howard Lake

AURELIAN INFORMATION UK

SPONSOR'S FOREWORD

It was a fortunate set of coincidences that originally put us in touch with Kim Worts at Aurelian Information. We had learned of Howard Lake's plans to publish his experiences and thought that it would be a great idea to sponsor the resulting book.

As yet, the Internet is a largely untapped medium for fundraising. Current estimates indicate that the Worldwide Internet Community is approximately 40 million people and growing at 10% per month. Encouragingly, the UK has one of the largest take-up rates outside of the USA.

Clearly, UK charities have an unprecedented opportunity to build an Internet presence which not only informs, but recruits donors and accepts donations directly. Furthermore, putting a charity's supporters on-line results in a way of communicating en masse with the donors at no cost. Through Direct Connection's affinity schemes a charity can also receive constant revenue based on numbers of members signed up.

The Internet is an environment which people can feel part of and within which each has a voice. We believe that this is important inside any organisation as well. At Direct Connection, we view the people who work for us as a family and the company is enriched by their varied experiences and opinions. This approach has created a dedicated team, a happy atmosphere at work which has filtered through to our customers. It was a natural step for us to develop close links with the Not-For-Profit Sector.

This book is an excellent introduction to the benefits of joining the Internet community. Howard Lake brings with him an impressive academic background and a wealth of experience both from his work with Amnesty International and the UK Internet Fundraising Web Site.

Direct Connection is delighted that Howard has written this book. We hope that it will set you thinking.

Trevor I. Diamond
Business Development Manager
Direct Connection
London, June 1996
trevord@dircon.co.uk

CONTENTS

Also from AURELIAN

WHO'S WHO IN THE VOLUNTARY SECTOR

This well-known annual national directory of over 1000 chief executives and other key figures and their organisations in the UK charity sector, details their current inter-charity and government roles, present and past committees, boards, trusteeships and professional backgrounds. PLUS: specially commissioned **articles by leading experts** on current charity management issues, a **directory of consultants and services** for charity managers *and* a **noticeboard of forthcoming training opportunities** for charity people at senior level - this unique networking reference source is now used by the voluntary, professional and commercial sectors nationwide.

Format: A4 Paperback, 196pp £ 45.00 Charity Discount Price £ 29.50

CHARITIES-ON-LINE - *EXPRESS*

The new high speed database reference source with its specially designed off-line reader is the fastest and most efficient way to access information on thousands of charities and trusts and other agencies in the UK.

Silver Level access with its special download facility tells you what the organisations do and where they are - with the very latest address/phone/fax details. *Gold Level* gives in-depth profiles of the organisations including named personnel, policy, income bands, number of staff, etc with mail merge facility. **CHARITIES-ON-LINE -** *EXPRESS* is designed for all users of voluntary and charity organisation information - in the commercial, academic, institutional and voluntary sectors. The special lawyers' facility LEGAL SCREEN identifies charities seeking funds from wills, legacies and new trusts.

Prices Ex VAT: Registration: £25.00
Annual Subscription: *Silver Level*: £100.00 *Gold Level* £225.00

ORDERS/ENQUIRIES: AURELIAN INFORMATION LTD - UK
TEL 0181-960 7918 FAX 0171-794 8609 E-MAIL aurelian@geo2.poptel.org.uk

1 INTRODUCTION

It takes vision to be thinking about the Internet now, but vision is not something we lack in the UK voluntary sector. The Internet is going to dramatically change the way we communicate with our supporters and donors in the coming years, just as much as direct mail and the telephone has done in the last ten.
Michael Johnston,
programme for *How to use the Internet*
October 1995

The Internet, the huge network of people communicating with each other via computers, is a vast marketplace where companies are doing business with other companies, people are buying services and products, and profits are being made. This marketplace is unlike any other because for the first time small businesses can rub shoulders on a level playing field with major multinationals in front of a global audience, all for the cost of a few hundred pounds a year.

Three years ago, just as the Internet first began to move into the public gaze, I wondered if charities were making use of this new opportunity. If people and companies were happy to do deals and part with money online, surely they would be happy to direct some of that money towards charities? But were charities online? Not very many of them. How many of them were asking for money? Hardly any.

I have spent the last three years researching into the possibilities of charities fundraising on the Internet. I am a professional fundraiser myself so I wanted to know if this was a valid new means of raising money. My conclusion is an emphatic yes, based on the pioneering efforts of a small number of fundraisers who have experimented with the new medium and learned from their mistakes.

I also wanted to know if the Internet could help me in my day-to-day fundraising work in any way. I was delighted to find that hundreds of other fundraisers were already online and communicating with each other daily. As well as this professional self-help network I came across hundreds of online information resources that were of use both to me and to my colleagues. Many of these were US-biased, it is true, but during 1995 the number of UK-specific resources grew considerably. All this information was available for free, on-demand and whenever I wanted it.

The Internet, therefore, is an extremely valuable resource to fundraisers working for charities large and small. In fact, as the small businesses on the Internet demonstrate, it is often the smaller organisations with a focused audience and niche market that are gaining most from their minimal investment in establishing an Internet presence.

The Internet now is easier and cheaper to join than ever. You probably don't need to invest in fancy new computer equipment and you don't have to leap in at the deep end with a fancy World Wide Web site. E-mail, the basic method of communication that links everyone on the Internet, is a perfectly effective fundraising tool on its own. So you can dip your toe and try out different fundraising ideas gradually if you prefer. Even if your charity does not use the Internet to make appeals with a World Wide Web page, you may well find that the fundraising information and advice you can tap into more than justifies your charity's use of the Internet.

The Internet is not "the answer" to your fundraising problems: indeed, for any solutions it offers it also creates new problems. It is, however, a significant and dynamic new tool for communicating with donors, carrying out research and improving your fundraising skills, knowledge and contacts.

This book is written by a fundraiser for fundraisers. It explains clearly how you can use the Internet in your fundraising work in many different ways. It does not go into unnecessary technical details or cover general information such as how to use the Internet, there are plenty of other books that cover those subjects. This is a guide for charity fundraisers whether they work full- or part-time, in a large international charity or in a small community group.

The book is full of examples of how other charities are using the Internet. Throughout the book there are plenty of Internet addresses listed in brackets like these "< >" so that, when you get Internet access yourself, you can go and see the example on the Internet. Internet addresses can change from time to time, so for the up-to-date list of addresses mentioned in this book, visit the UK Fundraising World Wide Web site <**http://www.fundraising.co.uk**>. This is a free resource that I have created for other charity fundraisers in the UK containing links to the many sites on the Internet of interest to fundraisers, based on my research. You will also find news of a new e-mail discussion list for UK fundraisers so that they can ask questions and share information with each other and provided by courtesy of Direct Connection Ltd. You are very welcome to join the list.

Howard Lake, London, May 1996

2 WHY GET ON THE INTERNET?

I believe the charity, voluntary or not-for-profit sector... will actually become a major beneficiary as our society moves towards the Net... I think causes of all types will discover the Net to be their most powerful fund-raising medium ever.

Ray Hammond, *Digital Business:*
Surviving and Thriving in an On-line World,
Hodder and Stoughton, 1996

The Internet is already being used by for-profit companies to do business in many different ways, from advertising their services, through selling products and carrying out market research, to providing value-added services to existing clients. It is now very much a marketplace where business-to-individual and business-to-business marketing are practised. Despite misleading newspaper stories about the "lack of security" of transmitting data on the Internet, people have been using it to buy and sell, including via credit card, for some time. Visa estimated that in 1994 there were around $200 million worth of credit-card transactions worldwide related to Internet business. An October 1995 survey found that about 14% of World Wide Web users, or 2.5 million people, had purchased products or services over the Internet **<http://www.commerce.net/information/surveys/exec_sum.html>**.

Money is being spent and made on the Internet. If it is a marketplace for for-profit companies, from small businesses to large corporations, then the Internet must also offer a marketplace for nonprofit organisations, from local community groups to international charities. The millions of potential customers whom the for-profits are trying to attract via their WWW sites are also potential supporters for many nonprofits.

Ken Burnett in *Relationship Fundraising* points to the valuable lessons charity fundraisers can learn from the for-profit sector. However, he argues that "*a fundraising transaction is fundamentally different to a commercial business transaction and while fundraisers have much to learn from commercial practice they will commit a fatal, suicidal, error if they embrace commercial practices too enthusiastically... To succeed in fundraising marketing [a fundraiser] has to adapt commercial marketing methods, not simply adopt them*".

The Internet is a communications tool, another channel by which people can contact people. The oft-quoted description of the Internet as a network of computer networks is misleading because it considers only the technology: The Internet is much more a network of people using computers to communicate with other people.

The Internet offers new methods of communicating with people, and therefore, from a fundraiser's point of view, of asking them to support a cause. Some of these communication methods have never before been possible in any other medium; e-mail, for example, exhibits characteristics of other types of communication such as fax, telephone conferencing, and informal conversation, but it is all these and more. Some of the Internet's methods of communication are good alternatives to existing media, and others are frankly not as good or as straightforward as current methods. Charities, and fundraisers in particular, will therefore have to select the appropriate media for their message and integrate them with their existing fundraising communications, matching each to their appropriate function.

Few charities will want to embrace all the communication tools available on the Internet as they will simply not be appropriate. Some charities might use only e-mail, whereas others may incorporate advanced World Wide Web sites with online chat areas and video magazines. There is no "right" or "standard" way in which to use the Internet to raise funds.

Charities are already online

Many charities do, of course, already use the Internet and electronic communications networks. Indeed, some have been using them for quite a while. It is quite possible that many fundraisers' colleagues in other departments such as the research department, press office, campaigns team, or field office use e-mail on a regular, perhaps daily, basis. It is worth asking around to find out if even one person in your charity already has access to the Internet as their experience might assist in convincing the board, or finance committee, of the business benefits already enjoyed by the charity.

Nonprofits have been using the Internet to organise and campaign for many years. The development during the 1980s of what went on to become the international Association for Progressive Communications enabled a number of nonprofits all round the world, in particular those engaged in environmental and human rights campaigns, to communicate cheaply via e-mail with their various offices nationally and internationally and with other nonprofits and grassroots organisations.

The Internet is now being used by many nonprofit organisations to publish information and to further their objectives through campaigning and public education. Many of the large campaigning organisations such as Amnesty International and Greenpeace have a long history of innovative use of telecommunications and electronic information. At the same time, the relatively low entry cost to using the Internet has enabled many smaller nonprofits and community organisations to conduct nationwide and even international campaigning actions which, using traditional publishing methods, would have been prohibitively expensive. For example, a variety of nonprofits have used the World Wide Web to help in their search for missing children including The Polly Klaas <http://www.northcoast.com/klaas/klaas.html>, the Samaritans have extended their telephone helpline service by developing a pioneering e-mail helpline, and Friends of the Earth have published information on industrial emissions <http://www.foe.co.uk/cri/index.html>.

The Internet is many things to many people. One thing it is not: it is not "the answer" to fundraisers' prayers, the magic technological fix that will standardise, automate and increase the efficiency of a charity's ability to generate income. It will not replace current, traditional and highly-refined methods of raising funds, such as direct mail and telemarketing. Nor should it be a new charity's first or only fundraising activity: the value of fundraising on the Internet is that it can build on a variety of "traditional" fundraising schemes. If your charity has a limited budget and is choosing between a direct mail appeal and a World Wide Web site, the direct mail appeal must be given priority. The Internet is not a luxury for fundraisers but it is not yet more lucrative than the tried-and-tested fundraising methods.

However, used appropriately and creatively, the Internet is already an invaluable additional tool to thousands of fundraisers in many aspects of their daily work. Like the humble telephone, it can be used for routine office work or, in the hands of a professional, it can be wielded as a powerful method of communicating with individual donors. Like the fax machine a few years back, the Internet is currently seen by some as a luxury for some charities. How many charities, however, can now function efficiently without their fax machine?

Given the endless demands placed on fundraisers to raise more money or find "new" money, the global communications revolution that has occurred in the last few years in the shape of the Internet surely demands experimentation. Fundraisers have tried direct mail, telemarketing, some have even tried Direct Response TV appeals - could the Internet be "the next big thing" in fundraising? Ken Burnett advised in *Relationship Fundraising* that *"fundraisers must be constantly vigilant to ensure no worthwhile avenues are overlooked"*.

Reasons to be online

Charities have many reasons to become proficient in using the Internet, but why should fundraisers in particular use the Internet? The following list is far from comprehensive but does demonstrate that the question is really: Can fundraisers afford *not* to use the Internet?

Fundraisers can:
- Raise new funds by making direct and indirect appeals to individuals, trusts and companies

- Raise new funds by selling merchandise, reports and other information

- Raise funds by encouraging existing donors who are online to upgrade their donations to tax-efficient or pledged giving

- Reach new, larger markets for a fraction of the cost of paper-based appeals

- Keep in regular contact with many more donors for a fraction of the cost of paper-based communications

Fundraisers can use the Internet to raise money while saving money. Almost all the fundraising material, such as text and graphics, used in Internet appeals will simply be recycled from existing fundraising material. Even better, many of the donations that they encourage can be made automatically from anywhere in the world. They can be made almost instantaneously with an automatic and similarly instantaneous acknowledgement, they do not require a fundraiser to be permanently at the end of a telephone, and the appeal costs can be kept in the region of hundreds rather than thousands of pounds.

So far, the reasons for being online have all included direct generation of income, which is fair enough, given the principal task of a fundraiser. These are the reasons that trustees or senior management will expect to see at the top of the list if they are to be convinced that fundraising on the Internet is to be attempted by their charity.

However, to see the Internet simply as an automatic money machine is to seriously underestimate its value to fundraisers and, indeed, to donors. The significance of the Internet to fundraisers lies much more, at the moment at least, in the myriad of ways in which it can assist and enhance their day-to-day fundraising work.

The Internet also offers fundraisers:
- Numerous free advice networks with other fundraisers from organisations large and small, in many different countries, who face the same or similar challenges. They are willing to share ideas and solutions free of charge in the hope that someone else will help them when they have a problem.

- Freely and instantly-available grant and funding information.

- Information on training courses, conferences, seminars and professional development opportunities.

- Information on suppliers, consultants and service organisations.

- A method of gathering market research information from donors and would-be donors, responding to their needs, and publicly acknowledging their support.

- A wide variety of resources to assist fundraising research, including company information on corporate donors, telephone/address look-up services, and various free news services.

Arguing that the Internet will help generate significant new income in the short term might not therefore be the most appropriate approach. However, it is quite possible that some charities which do not use the Internet to seek donations will still conclude that there is a sound business reason for providing Internet access to its fundraisers in order to use it for research, donor communication, and networking with other fundraisers.

One online, all online

"There is no doubt your organisation has to get on-line. There are just too many people on the Internet now and in the future to ignore"
Michael Johnston,
Professional Fundraising magazine, September 1995.

Whilst there are compelling reasons for fundraisers to develop an Internet presence, no fundraiser should attempt to do so alone within their organisation. A charity World Wide Web site that consists of nothing more than a fundraising appeal will look out of place. It will probably perform as badly as a direct mail appeal to donors or members that asks for money but fails to include background details on what the charity is doing and why it needs the money.

In other words, the full range of a charity's activities should be presented when it develops an Internet presence. This applies whether the charity has a World Wide Web site or is simply offering an e-mail address. Why, for example, offer e-mail access to the membership/donor services department if an external enquirer cannot reach the press office by the same method? Charities do not offer supporters telephone access to some departments and not to others.

A charity, therefore, should acquire an online presence on an organisation-wide basis. Even if fundraisers believe that they need an Internet presence as soon as possible, they must first convince the rest of their charity to join them.

Needless to say, given the novelty of the Internet and charities' lack of experience with the medium, very few of the first charities to move online followed this precept. Nor, indeed, did all for-profit organisations for that matter. A visit to virtually any UK charity's World Wide Web site in 1994 and 1995 would have revealed an abundance of press releases and project reports but no indication that the charity required financial assistance, and certainly no direct requests for donations. Clearly, the press/public affairs departments, or in some cases the IT departments, had controlled the development and content of the Web sites and had failed, whether intentionally or not, to include the fundraising or marketing departments in their planning. The result was that most charity World Wide Web sites looked rather unbalanced, offering a distorted representation of the organisation's activities and needs to visitors.

So, it might well frustrate the fundraiser eager to experiment with online fundraising, but from the charity's standpoint it is undoubtedly better to wait until the organisation as a whole is ready to move online.

Convinced of the need to use the Internet, or at least to test its effectiveness, fundraisers next have to set about gaining access to it.

Further information

For a summary of the issues involved in deciding why to get on to the Internet, Impact Online provide useful assistance in their Internet 101 guide at **<http://www.impactonline.org/words/internet/index.html>**

A list of reasons why charities should use the Internet, based on actual experience, is included in the soc.org.nonprofit newsgroup's FAQ (part 11) at **<http://www.eskimo.com/~pbarber/npo-faq-p11.html#chapter1.3>** and some specific reasons for fundraisers to use the Internet are detailed at **<http://www.eskimo.com/~pbarber/npo-faq-p11.html#chapter1.11>**.

Summary

- The Internet is already a marketplace for small businesses and large corporations.

- People are spending money on the Internet in large numbers.

- Successful fundraisers will adapt rather than adopt commercial Internet marketing methods.

- The Internet offers a significant new marketing channel for fundraisers.

- Many charities already have a long history of using the Internet for campaigning and coordination.

- Fundraisers can use the Internet to raise funds from individuals, companies, and foundations.

- Fundraisers can use the Internet to communicate with existing and potential donors at minimal cost.

- Fundraisers can use the Internet to share the advice and expertise of thousands of other fundraisers around the world.

- A fundraising Internet presence on its own will perform badly: the whole charity must have an online presence, otherwise the organisation will look unbalanced to a visitor.

3 HOW TO GET ON THE INTERNET

Being on the Internet can mean a whole host of things to different people, from having a CompuServe account at home to running a World Wide Web server computer from within your charity's offices. Technically, you are on the Internet if you can make contact via e-mail from your computer with other computers which have Internet addresses e.g. yourname@charityname.org.

If you cannot, then you may still have an e-mail system that connects the computers in your office. But it will be a closed system. In other words, you cannot use it to connect to the outside world. Fortunately, it is a cheap technical matter to fit a gateway box that will give you this link.

For the purposes of this book, getting on to the Internet is taken to mean acquiring access to the main methods of sending and receiving information via the Internet, namely e-mail, telnet, FTP (File Transfer Protocol), Usenet, IRC (Internet Relay Chat) and the World Wide Web, and perhaps a few other services such as Ping. Access to these methods of transferring information over the Internet will enable you to conduct all the fundraising activities covered in this book. Fortunately, they are becoming a fairly standard package from all companies offering access to the Internet. As a fundraiser you might well not end up using all of them in your fundraising work, but it is still useful to know that they are available. Encouragingly, it is possible to access almost all the features of the Internet using e-mail alone (see Chapter 4), and it is as well to remember that many people in the world who have access to the Internet can only do so with e-mail.

Getting wired without the wires

Before covering the different ways of getting on to the Internet, it should be pointed out that it is possible to have an Internet presence without being online yourself. This can be in the form of a World Wide Web page (or pages) created for your charity by someone else. This could be someone you have paid or a volunteer or supporter with the requisite skills and access who has done it free of charge. In this situation your charity will have a World Wide Web site address, or a Universal Resource Locator ("URL"), such as <http://www.charityname.org>, but it will not have an e-mail address, such as name@charityname.org.

Certainly, that is how many small charities test the waters of the Internet and it is worth considering as a cheap, and in some cases free, first step. There are, however, a number of disadvantages. The most significant is simply that your charity is not contactable via the Internet. Any information on your Web page about how to contact you will necessarily omit the all-important e-mail address. The only way a visitor to your page could contact you is via the telephone or fax or letter: that will probably be expensive if they live outside your region or country, difficult if they are in another time zone, or just rather slow. Without an e-mail address the magic circle of instant response that the Internet affords is broken, and fundraisers already know that income from appeals can be significantly affected if even one small obstacle is placed in the way of the would-be donor.

Having an Internet presence without having Internet access yourself will make you rely entirely on the company or individual posting your information. If it is a commercial relationship then you will have some redress. If not, however, what control will you have over how the information is presented? Will the company or individual promote your site on the Internet? If so, how and where? Will they do so responsibly? How quickly can they update the page? What sort of page access statistics do they provide?

This sounds like looking a gift-horse in the mouth and a number of charities will no doubt report that they were able to benefit considerably from such a free toe-dipping exercise. Yet this hands-off situation must remain temporary, not least because effective fundraising on the Internet involves far more than simply putting up a World Wide Web page.

That said, in the UK there are a number of companies which are either Internet Service Providers or World Wide Web publishers in some form and are happy to provide free World Wide Web space for charities. These include Future Publishing Ltd <**http://www.futurenet.co.uk**>, MarketNet <**http://mkn.co.uk**>, and Internet-UK <**http://www.uk-charities.org/charity.htm**>. FutureNet's offer has been taken up, for example, by the Adult Dyslexia Organisation and Freecare, both of whom include an appeal for funds on their pages. Direct Connection <**sales@dircon.co.uk**> encourages charities to use the Internet by offering an affinity marketing scheme, with which it will donate £10 per annum to selected participating charities for every member or donor who takes out an individual subscription. Internet facilities including websites are provided free of charge for those charities with whom Direct Connection is working closely.

The Contact Center provides an international list of organisations offering free or low cost space for non-profit or community web sites at <**http://www.contact.org/orgs/frspace.htm**>. It might be daunting to realise that your choice has truly expanded from the national to international level, but it has proved useful for some charities. For example, St Georges Romania Appeal, which is based in Weybridge in Surrey, England, has chosen to store its Web pages on the computer server of nonprofit.net in the USA.

A different option for charities wishing to publish information on the World Wide Web and to promote their activities are the services provided by organisations such as OneWorld Online <**http://www.oneworld.org**> and VOIS <**http://www.vois.org.uk**>. These are two nonprofit organisations which have set out to be "supersites" or "primary presences" for nonprofits. In other words they provide a central site where visitors can find information provided by a number of charities. With major nonprofits such as Oxfam and Amnesty International UK publishing their information on OneWorld Online, smaller or less well-known charities can benefit from being listed with them on the same site. OneWorld Online has now developed a reputation as one of the leading Internet resources for nonprofits working on international development issues, and VOIS is now positioning itself as the leading general site for UK charities.

Both organisations charge charities for publishing their information on the sites. OneWorld Online take care of translating a nonprofit's text to Hypertext Markup Language ("HTML") for use in a Web page while VOIS encourages charities themselves to do so using an easy-to-use template supplied on disk or interactively via a form for pages already stored on the site.

OneWorld Online was originally unable to allow charities on its site to engage in any fundraising or commercial activities due to the restrictions of its host.

These restrictions no longer apply following the addition of a second independent server and some of the charities on OneWorld Online are now including fundraising activities on their pages. VOIS has been keen from the beginning to allow charities to engage in fundraising.

Making the connection

If you wish to use the Internet and be contactable via it, rather than simply have a World Wide Web page stored by someone else, you need various pieces of equipment and services. Some you probably already have, others you will have to buy - or you might be able to acquire them as donations.

To get connected to the Internet you will need a personal computer with some spare space on the hard drive, a modem, and a telephone line. Is your computer good enough to connect to the Internet? Almost certainly. However, while various enthusiasts can rig even ten-year-old computers up to the Internet, the general rule is that computers made in the last two or three years can provide good enough service if used to access the Internet. So PCs that are 386s or better will do, and Pentiums will do even better. For those running Macs, 68030 processors or better are fine for using the Internet. The general rule is that the newer the computer and the faster its processing speed the better access you will get to the Internet and the less it will cost in terms of remaining online. So, if you're lucky enough to have Pentiums and Windows95 or PowerPCs and MacOS then you will usually enjoy good access speeds. At the same time, those charities which do not have the latest equipment, ie almost all of them, should not feel that they are bound to upgrade in order to gain access to the Internet.

The size of RAM, the computer's operating memory, is an important consideration. Most computers today are sold with at least eight megabytes of RAM. To access the Internet you need not buy extra RAM but it might be helpful if you wish to have more than one software program open at the same time. Twelve megabytes might be more reliable.

Modems are the hardware boxes that translate computers' digital data into a format that will travel along non-digital telephone lines and then reconvert it when it arrives at the destination computer. There is far more of a case for buying the fastest you can afford here. At present, 28.8K (28,800 Kilobytes per second of data transfer) is becoming standard, replacing the 14.4K speed modem. The extra cost, currently in the region of £50 or less, is worth it in terms of reduced telephone bills. The faster the data travels back to your computer the less time you need to remain connected to the Internet via the telephone line.

Given the infinite varieties of software, hardware and organisational uses of computers, the above can be no more than a general guide. Consult your IT supplier, your IT officer if you have one, or pick up one of the many Internet-related magazines now available. *Internet* and *.net* are two reliable and useful UK-based magazines that should give you a better idea of the type of equipment you might need.

One other general rule, if you are starting to use the Internet it might be best not to run it from the computer that houses the charity's donor base. This is not so much a question of the hordes of hackers that the media leads us to believe are waiting breathlessly to steal our data as soon as we send our first e-mail message, but simply good practice. The fundraiser accessing the Internet from the computer will probably be taking up a fair amount of time sitting at the machine, particularly while getting used to it - thereby perhaps excluding others from the essential day-to-day maintenance of the donor base and other computer-based activities. In larger charities, especially those linked via a network, this will not be an issue, but in smaller organisations with fewer than half a dozen computers it is worth considering.

Internet Service Providers (ISPs)

Once you have the necessary equipment, you must then purchase access to the Internet. Simply connecting the modem to the telephone socket is not enough.

The basic level of getting on to the Internet involves access via a dial-up account. In other words, using computer software, you dial the telephone number of a certain central computer that then gives you access to the Internet for as long as you wish, until you disconnect using the software. While you are connected you can send, receive and search for information on the Internet. This dial-up service will typically cost your charity about £30 to establish, plus £10-15 per month. You will also have to pay the telephone charges that you will incur whilst connected, but as you are only ever connected to a local telephone number your calls will be charged at local rates, even if you are retrieving information from a computer on the other side of the world. Although there is no typical rate of use of the Internet by a charity, an account for one person will probably cost around £350 per year.

There are over 120 companies in the UK offering access to the Internet. They are known as Internet Service Providers or ISPs, and more companies appear every month. These are in addition to the commercial online services such as America Online, CompuServe and Europe Online. It is impossible to recommend an ideal service for a fundraising charity, not least because the price deals and services offered change frequently. In general, though, you need to ask the following questions when choosing a provider:

- How much does it cost per person per month to have an Internet account that offers e-mail, World Wide Web, Usenet, FTP, telnet and IRC access?

- How much more does it cost to add another person from the same charity, ie with a different e-mail address?

- What is the one-off set-up charge to open this account?

- Are there any online charges in addition to telephone connection charges? Most ISPs make no charge per minute, but commercial online services do.

- Does the ISP support your type of computer? Not all ISPs support Macintoshes.

- Is the software provided by the ISP already registered or is it shareware? If it is not registered then you will probably have to pay extra to use it legally. Some Internet software packages' licences state that they are free for use by staff of nonprofit organisations.

- What is the ISP's modem-to-user ratio? In other words, how many other account holders might be trying to dial in to the system at the same time as you? Somewhere around 1:20 is tolerable.

- What is the ISP's average downtime? Most ISP's central computers are unavailable for short periods every month, which can cause frustration. An independent analysis of top ISPs' figures is published in *Internet* magazine each month.

- What percentage of the country does the ISP cover? Can you dial in to them from anywhere in the country via a Point of Presence (PoP) access point at local telephone call rates?

- Can the ISP offer 28.8K access from all its PoPs? If not, look elsewhere.

- Do you need the special content available on a commercial on-line service such as CompuServe, ie train timetables, stocks and shares information, and roadwork updates, as well as the information available on the Internet? If the answer is yes, then you will need to select the appropriate online service rather than simply an Internet Service Provider.

- What benefits can the ISP offer charities? Do you, for example, receive free World Wide Web space? If so, how much in terms of disk space? 0.5Mb is just about acceptable, but 5Mb would be better.

- What kind of access do you get to your World Wide Web space? Can you FTP files to your directory and do you get script/Common Gateway Interface (CGI) access? These questions may not be relevant at first but they will indi-

14

cate how much flexibility you can expect if or when you develop a World Wide Web site that is anything other than a static noticeboard. A "yes" would be an encouraging sign.

This list is necessarily brief. For a broader understanding of the issues involved in selecting an ISP, look at a copy of an Internet magazine. They regularly include information on what you need to know to get online.

A number of ISPs have close links to the UK voluntary sector. GreenNet <**http://www.gn.apc.org**> provides access to a range of environmental, peace and human rights nonprofits as well as individuals interested in these issues. As well as Internet access, subscribers get access to international discussion fora on these subjects (including one on fundraising). Poptel <**http://www.pop-tel.org.uk/** > "aims to 'connect, inform, empower' by enabling information exchange. We collaborate in projects to make telematics widely accessible to the local and global community, and provide on-line information systems to trades unions, campaigns, agencies, charities and organisations". Direct Connection host a number of major charity websites and are committed to developing closer ties to the voluntary sector with affinity membership incentive schemes and linked services.

If you are still undecided about choosing an ISP, ask charities that are already online if they would recommend their ISP. The Charity Forum <charityforum@geo2.poptel.org.uk>, an umbrella organisation of over 400 UK charities, is currently researching member charities' experiences with ISPs for use as a guide to those selecting an ISP.

It is also likely that over a period of time you will move to another ISP that meets your needs better. This should not cause too many problems. So, even if you find you have not made the right decision at the beginning - and from the comments on UK newsgroups from dissatisfied customers of ISPs you won't be alone - you can change to a more suitable one when you are ready.

The in-house solution

Charities that are heavy users of the Internet can also bring much of the system in-house. This is a costly investment, not least because it requires hiring skilled staff to run the system. The necessary equipment is expensive too, particularly if it is to cope with heavy use both by staff within the charity and by external users. A charity which decides to set up and run its own World Wide Web server in-house will also have to pay for a permanent leased line so that visitors can access the site 24 hours a day. At present this method might cost about £50,000-£100,000.

Certainly such a large-scale approach is the best solution for some nonprofits. Friends of the Earth **<http://www.foe.co.uk>**, for example, run their own World Wide Web site in-house, but they did manage to reduce their costs by acquiring a computer server as a donation from Sun Microsystems. Even if you do decide to run an in-house server, you will still need to pay for access to the Internet through an ISP.

Other information

For a list of Internet Service Providers look in the back of *NetUser* magazine. Alternatively a list of UK and Ireland Internet Service Providers is maintained at **<http://www.limitless.co.uk/inetuk/providers.html>** and a searchable list of more than 1,900 Internet Service Providers at **<http://www.thelist.com>**. These are, of course, only of any use if you, or someone you know, already has access to the Internet.

Summary

- "Getting on the Internet" means having access to Internet facilities such as e-mail, telnet, FTP (File Transfer Protocol), Usenet, IRC (Internet Relay Chat) and the World Wide Web.

- Try out an Internet presence free of charge or at low cost with a World Wide Web page on someone else's computer.

- A free Internet presence is not, however, going to help you in the long-run: you will need to get and pay for Internet access for your charity.

- To access the Internet you need a computer, a modem, a telephone line and an account with an Internet Service Provider.

- Find out whether the Internet Service Provider will provide you with the breadth and quality of service you want. If you make a mistake it is very easy to move to a more suitable Provider.

4 COMMUNICATING WITH OTHER FUNDRAISERS

Folklore is an important part of [a profession or discipline], consisting of idiosyncratic information about how equipment really works and what tricks you have to know to get the experiment to come out right. It never appears in journal articles or manuals, and it is typically conveyed by word of mouth. With electronic communication, folklore can be more broadly accessible.

L Sproull and S Kiesler,
Connections: New Ways of Working in the Networked World,
MIT Press, 1991

Both novice and experienced fundraisers need to ask for help or advice at some time. The Internet offers access to a valuable and extensive resource of free advice from fellow fundraisers on almost all aspects of fundraising on and off the Internet. Not surprisingly, there is a great deal of discussion on the Internet about the possibilities of fundraising on the Internet itself.

Asking for help from other fundraisers: the value of e-mail lists

As much fundraising relies on commonsense and not reinventing the wheel, fundraisers often like to discuss ideas with other fundraisers, whether colleagues or counterparts in other organisations. For the solo or part-time fundraiser in small organisations this contact is even more essential. Hence the popularity of conferences and seminars. However, valuable as these are, they can be expensive and they only last a few days at most. E-mail offers a very effective and cheap method of keeping in contact with other fundraisers throughout the year.

E-mail is very useful for sending cheap messages from one person to another, but to post a question to a large group of fundraisers you would have to find out their individual e-mail addresses, a time-consuming task. A much easier method is to join an e-mail discussion list on a fundraising subject. This is an online "discussion" between anything from two to two thousand fundraisers. On a list any member can send a question to everyone else on the list for the minimal cost of sending a single e-mail. Compare that to the cost of telephoning or faxing several hundred fundraisers! The software that automates these lists then copies each message to everyone else on the list. Any response to the query from anyone on the list is then similarly distributed to everyone else on the list, and an ongoing 'discussion' has begun. E-mail lists will usually have several discussions or 'threads' continuing at the same time.

Although one "subscribes" to an e-mail list there is no payment involved. To subscribe one simply sends a simple message to the list's e-mail address. The request is processed automatically and shortly afterwards a confirmation message is received and then the first postings start to arrive.

What e-mail lists are available to fundraisers?

US fundraisers have been using e-mail discussion lists since at least 1989. As a result they have a well-developed range of lists covering a variety of topics (see below). Almost all of these have been created by fundraisers for fundraisers so the emphasis is very much on self-help. Every list has a clearly defined topic for discussion and messages off that subject are discouraged.

Most lists are run by university fundraisers because they have easy access to their universities' computer systems and services, which have been the hub of the Internet for decades. So in practice fundraisers can thank the universities for picking up the bill for actually running these lists (and thank the list managers who have to deal with all the administrative problems behind the scenes). However, anyone can run an e-mail list, even from their home PC, at very little cost.

Fundraising discussion lists can be public, allowing anyone, even non-fundraisers to subscribe, or private where subscription depends on paying a fee or on proving your professional status. Lists are either unmoderated, allowing subscribers to post any message they want, or moderated by a list-owner, to ensure that messages are relevant and acceptable. Lists can allow conversations or they can be one-way only: in the latter case an individual, or in most cases an organisation, can send regular messages and announcements to subscribers. Lists can be small and private too: one group of five US researchers have set up their own e-mail list to discuss aspects of a software package that they use regularly. Anyone with e-mail can do something like this: most e-mail packages let you set up a mailing list so that every time you select the list name you automatically send to the dozen or so people you want to receive the message. It is only when lists get beyond this homely size that you need to invest in some automatic list software such as listserv or majordomo.

All the e-mail lists presented here are available for public subscription. Fundraisers should not be surprised if only one or two are relevant to their precise area of work: one of the lists' main strengths is that they are very focused.

US AND CANADA-BASED FUNDRAISING DISCUSSION LISTS

The following lists are of particular interest, for each their own description of the subject they deal with has been reproduced. To subscribe send the message as set out for each below (substitute your names for "Firstname Lastname") to the list's e-mail address.

CDN-GIFTPL-L - to facilitate the exchange of information, ideas and questions regarding Canadian charitable gift planning.
Message: SUBSCRIBE CDN-GIFTPL-L Firstname Lastname
e-mail address: listproc@listserv.mcmaster.ca
unmoderated; no FAQ available;
List's WWW site/archives: none

CFRNET - addresses those involved in building partnerships between educational institutions and corporations and foundations.
Message: Subscribe cfrnet Firstname Lastname
e-mail address: listserv@unc.edu
unmoderated; no FAQ available;
List's WWW site/archives: none

FUNDCAN - for educational fundraisers working within the Canadian context. It is limited to topics related to fundraising in the educational field in particular.
Message: Subscribe FundCan Firstname Lastname
e-mail address: listserv@qucdn.queensu.ca
unmoderated; no FAQ available;
List's WWW site/archives: none

FUNDLIST - the discussion of university fundraising issues.
Message: Sub fundlist Firstname Lastname
e-mail address: listproc@listproc.hcf.jhu.edu
unmoderated; no FAQ available;
List's WWW site/archives: http://davis.uri.edu

FUNDSVCS - for fundraising services technical discussions... Fundsvcs is more "nuts & bolts oriented".
Message: Subscribe fundsvcs
e-mail address: majordomo@acpub.duke.edu
unmoderated; no FAQ available;
List's WWW site/archives: ftp://development.duke.edu/ftp/guest/fundsvcs

GIFT-PL -for the exchange of information related to the field of charitable gift planning (run by the National Council on Planned Giving).
Message: Subscribe gift-pl Firstname Lastname
e-mail address: listserv@indycms.iupui.edu
unmoderated; no FAQ available;
List's WWW site/archives: none

GRANTS-L - to promote external funding for international education and research...
for sharing experience, ideas, thoughts, comments and sources of information on the
preparation and administration of contracts and grants.
Message: Subscribe GRANTS-L Firstname Lastname
e-mail address: listproc@listproc.gsu.edu
moderated; no FAQ available;
List's WWW site/archives: none

GRANTWRITER-L - for people interested in funding, grants and scholarships.
Message: Subscribe Grantwriter-L Firstname Lastname
e-mail address: majordomo@fallingrock.com
moderated; no FAQ available;
List's WWW site/archives: none

GRANTWRK -a group of people, from both the public and private sectors, who will
WORK together to improve the grants process. This will not be a listing of grant
sources, nor will it offer tips or suggestions on how to obtain grants.
Message: subscribe grantwrk
e-mail address: listserv@iubvm.ucs.indiana.edu
unmoderated; no FAQ available;
List's WWW site/archives: none

HILAROS - to support and encourage Christians in fundraising and discuss ideas and
issues from a Christian perspective.
Message: subscribe hilaros
e-mail address: majordomo@mark.geneva.edu
unmoderated; no FAQ available;
List's WWW site/archives: none

PRSPCT-L - discussions, announcements and queries regarding prospect research,
fundraising and related matters.
Message: Subscribe prspct-l Firstname Lastname
e-mail address: listserv@bucknell.edu
unmoderated; FAQ available;
List's WWW site/archives: gopher://listserv.cwis.uci.edu

It should be noted that list addresses do occasionally change, particularly if the
list owner changes jobs and moves to another organisation. For a current listing of lists and their addresses visit the UK Fundraising World Wide Web site
at <**http://www.fundraising.co.uk**>.

In addition to these lists, there are a number of others that are subscribed to by
other fundraisers and which often carry fundraising-related discussions. These
include:

US AND CANADA-BASED GENERAL NONPROFIT DISCUSSION LISTS OF INTEREST TO FUNDRAISERS

GIVING - for donors and volunteers who support nonprofit organisations (including those who give small financial contributions) and others interested in philanthropy and volunteer activity. It also covers appropriate fundraising expenses and asset size, executive compensation, excessive solicitations, donor motivations, and the ethics of giving. The list owner hopes "that donors and volunteers will use the list to engage in dialog which improves our understanding and judgement of the nonprofit sector and individual organisations in ways that will help us decide what to give and to whom".
Message: Subscribe giving Firstname Lastname
e-mail address: listproc@envirolink.org
unmoderated; no FAQ available;
List's WWW site/archives: none

Nonprofit-net - the use of the internet by nonprofit organisations
(run by Hubris Communications)
Message: sub nonprofit-net Firstname Lastname
e-mail address: listproc@nonprofit.net
unmoderated; no FAQ available;
List's WWW site/archives: http://www.nonprofit.net/listproc/archives/nonprofit-net/

TALK-AMPHILREV... a kind of "superlist", in the sense that it is intended to be a "large tent" that will encourage discussions across lines that usually separate the professions, disciplines, and sub-disciplines involved in the nonprofit arena, and across the "great divide" that separates the nonprofit sector from the for-profit sector that serves it. [Run by American Philanthropy Review]
Message: Subscribe talk-amphilrev Firstname Lastname
e-mail address: majordomo@tab.com
unmoderated; no FAQ available;
List's WWW site/archives: none

USnonprofit-l - a discussion group for issues facing nonprofit organisations, and the causes and people that they serve. Sponsored by the Santa Barbara RAIN Network in Santa Barbara, California.
Message: subscribe [in Subject: line]
e-mail address: usnonprofit-l-request@rain.org
unmoderated; FAQ available;
List's WWW site/archives: none

There are also many other specialist discussion lists to which certain types of fundraisers subscribe. For example, planned-giving fundraisers have GIFT-PL but might also subscribe to ESTPLAN-L (on estate planning) and the American Bar Association's Real Property, Probate and Trust Law list (ABA-RPPTL-GEN). Prospect researchers have PRSPCT-L but could also subscribe to ROOTS-L on genealogical research.

COMMERCIAL SUPPLIERS' LISTS FOR FUNDRAISERS

Commercial organisations which supply services or information to fundraisers are increasingly using e-mail lists, both for discussion and for distributing product or service information. Some have created lists for clients only while others have made them available to everyone. Blackbaud Inc, for example, has created the RE: Forum list that is available only for clients of its The Raiser's Edge database.

Fundraising and nonprofit sector magazines are using e-mail lists. *The Chronicle of Philanthropy* provides a free biweekly summary of the next issue's contents, including specific feature articles on management, technology and fundraising. It also provides a list of upcoming grant deadlines, which include details on the grant-making foundations' objects and the named correspondent for proposals. At the same time subscribers to the list receive a digest of events and training courses, divided by region. This information is available free of charge and is not restricted to paid subscribers to the paper version of *The Chronicle of Philanthropy.*

Falling Rock Software Co <**http://fallingrock.com**>, producers of Grant Writers Assistant, provides two lists, grantwriter-l and foundation-l. Grantwriter-l is a *"free service for people interested in funding, grants and scholarships as a way for us to share information with you, and for you to share information with others who share the same interest in grants"*. Foundation-l is a one-way list, providing a daily featured foundation from their records, with extensive details on address, financial balance sheet, etc.

While most lists are intended to run indefinitely, others are temporary in that they are set up for a specific one-off purpose. *Currents*, the membership magazine of CASE, the Council for Advancement and Support of Education, runs a monthly "Ask the Expert" list for two or three days. For the duration of each list, one or more experts is available from 9-5pm (EST) to answer questions from participants. "Ask the Expert" began in January 1995 and discussion topics have included planned giving and alumni development software.

US AND CANADA-BASED FUNDRAISING DISCUSSION LISTS PROVIDED BY FOR-PROFIT ORGANISATIONS

CASE CURRENTS' ASK THE EXPERT - covers a variety of topics, run by the Council for Advancement of Science and Education
Message: subscribe Firstname Lastname
e-mail address: author-request@ns.case.org
unmoderated; no FAQ available;
List's WWW site/archives: none

CHRONICLE OF PHILANTHROPY- preview of the newspaper, plus grant deadlines, events and training course listings
Message: Subscribe chronicle Firstname Lastname Organisation
e-mail address: chronicle-request@nonprofit.com
moderated/one-way; no FAQ available;
List's WWW site/archives: none

FOUNDATION-L - information on foundations and other funding resources.
Message: Subscribe foundation-l Firstname Lastname
e-mail address: majordomo@fallingrock.com
unmoderated/one-way; no FAQ available;
List's WWW site/archives: http://fallingrock.com

Not all lists succeed. INTFUND, a discussion list on international university
fundraising, was withdrawn during 1995 due to low subscriber levels.
However, many areas of fundraising activity are not yet covered by a discussion list so it is likely that the number of lists will grow. FUNDLIST has
already given birth to FUNDSVCS. A Special Events list has been proposed
on several occasions and might be available soon. Similarly, specialist groups
of fundraisers are setting up their own private discussion lists. For example
PRADO is a list available only to the Public Radio Association of
Development Officers, and PTV-DCOM is available only to Development and
Communications Personnel in Public Broadcast TV.

UK FUNDRAISING DISCUSSION LISTS
UK fundraisers are not as fortunate as their North American counterparts.
There are only two e-mail lists created for them, and the main list, ADMIN-
DEVELOP, is restricted to those fundraisers working in UK universities. A
second list was established by university rag societies to enable them to swap
information and best practice. It was intended from the beginning that charity
fundraisers would be invited to join the list, but this has not yet happened.

ADMIN-DEVELOP - for communication and information distribution, for sharing
news of impending developments, for offering opinions and for exchanging ideas
between CVCP and those responsible for UK university development, fundraising
and alumni relations. (Run by the Committee of Vice-Chancellors and Principals)
Message: [A message asking to join].
e-mail address: admin-develop-request@mailbase.ac.uk
unmoderated; no FAQ available;
For archives: Send index admin-develop to mailbase@mailbase.ac.uk

Although there are so few UK-focused lists, the North American fundraising
lists are available to fundraisers anywhere in the world. Although a few of the
lists are intended to be restricted to discussing issues relating to a single coun-

try, such as Canada's FUNDCAN and the USA's GIFT-PL, there is nothing stopping fundraisers from elsewhere subscribing and taking part in discussions. It is true that the subject matter of the fundraising discussion lists is very US-dominated. This is partially because almost all of the lists originated in the US for a US audience, but it is also because so few fundraisers from abroad have subscribed and added an international flavour. Nevertheless, many of the fundraising issues discussed are on such generic subjects that they are of relevance to fundraisers internationally.

How do fundraisers use the lists?

"Need a penny, take a penny. Have a penny, leave a penny." (From a sign on the counter of the general store near my home.) My translation: Need some info from this list, take freely. Have some information that's needed, give freely!"

Stephen C. Nill, J.D. (scnishere@aol.com) on GIFT-PL, 1995

Fundraisers use the lists for two fundamental reasons - to find information and to share information. Although the fundraising discussion lists cover different topics, there are five distinct types of message that appear on them:

- a question or request for information
- a response or answer
- an ongoing discussion
- an announcement of a new information resource (online or hard copy)
- job vacancy announcements

Typical messages include those checking to see if anyone else has already tried out a particular fundraising plan; networking with fundraisers with similar skills, geographical backgrounds or professional concerns; and discussing professional ethical concerns.

The free sharing of information on such a wide scale is perhaps surprising in a profession which is in theory competitive. Fundraisers are often approaching the same donors so to share information could lead to loss of competitive advantage. Yet the "gift economy" of the Internet applies to the fundraising lists as well, fostering a sense of online community. After a while, subscribers get to recognise regular posters, and gauge whose messages are more reliable, and whose advice is worth taking. This sense of community is real: fundraisers on the lists might be separated by hundreds of miles but some of them make the effort to meet up physically at conferences.

The level of co-operation and DIY self-help is remarkable. PRSPCT-L subscribers receive a monthly copy of the Internet Prospector, an extensive list of online resources of use to fundraising and prospect researchers. The publication is researched and edited by a team of volunteers on the list. On CFRNET in early 1996 an equally practical example of co-operation was established when it was suggested that subscribers review each other's grant proposals. The suggestion evoked a considerable response with over 60 people volunteering to join the proposal review group.

Occasionally a mistake is made and fundraisers cringe or commiserate: one list for example carried a personal message sent by mistake mentioning the poster's "boss from hell". The boss was another subscriber to the list, and the original message was followed by a very embarrassed apology. On another list subscribers saw a fundraiser's reference to psychiatric patients as "crazies" in a private message posted by mistake to the list: the poster apologised to the list after receiving a number of rebukes.

For those who think e-mail lists are too impersonal, there is the story of an American fundraiser who needed financial help for a bone marrow transplant. A request for funds from fellow professionals was made via FUNDLIST in the summer of 1994. A number of fundraisers clearly made personal donations in response because the original poster subsequently thanked those on the list who had helped when he announced in 1995 that the fundraiser had died the day before.

Tips on using e-mail lists

Joining e-mail lists means taking the time to read the messages and occasionally sending replies: in other words it gives you more work to do. Every message will not be relevant to your needs, so you will have to scroll through quite a few before you come across that valuable nugget.

The following are some practical suggestions on how best to benefit from fundraising e-mail lists.

- Do not subscribe to all the lists in one go or you might be overwhelmed with messages. Select the list that seems most relevant to you and subscribe. Get a feel for how busy the list is and how relevant it is for your work before you decide to subscribe to another. Find out if an FAQ, a list of Frequently Asked Questions and their answers, is available to help you avoid asking often-repeated questions.

- Do not send a message to the list straight away. Wait to get a feel for the quality of the list, its tone and the type of messages posted. Subscribers to the list expect focused fundraising information and discussions. Lists have an enduring memory of people who abuse the list or post irrelevant messages.

- Be polite and professional. Many lists' contributions are archived and available for searching so a libellous comment remains available to haunt you. You are also assumed to be speaking on behalf of your charity when you post, particularly if your signature includes its name and address. If you are speaking personally, say so.

- Switch to "digest format" using a simple e-mail message command to the list's software. This, and other useful commands should be included in the introduction to the list which you receive upon being successfully subscribed. This will ensure that you get a single daily message containing all messages sent to the list that day, rather than the 20 or 30 separate messages some lists generate. It is much easier to scroll through one file.

- Always keep a copy of the welcome message received on successfully subscribing. It will explain how to unsubscribe to the list. You will not be popular if you have to ask the list members how to unsubscribe.

- Always include a signature to your messages with your name, organisation, e-mail address and perhaps telephone number and postal address. This helps other subscribers know who is posting the message.

- Be careful with humorous messages: a joke does not always come across well in terse e-mail messages, and humour does not always travel well internationally.

- Do not be surprised if robust arguments develop. Occasionally lists erupt into disputes between two or more people on a particular professional issue. Either enjoy it or use the delete key.

- Do not advertise. Almost all the fundraising lists object to direct selling or advertising. Consultants and suppliers are usually welcome to join the lists, but should only provide relevant information to questions, and if necessary follow up with individuals off the list. (The only list that expressly permits, even encourages, such postings is TALK-AMPHILREV).

- Do not post "me too" messages. If someone offers a report or other resource do not reply to the list but to the individual who posted the offer. Several dozen "please send it to me as well" messages are of no use to the list subscribers. Some fundraisers pay personally for each message received so make each message count.

- Be concise.

- Quote appropriately from previous messages if you are replying to one so that other readers can follow the discussion.

- Try to read your e-mail messages at the beginning and end of the day. It is easy to get distracted and reply to messages as they arrive. Using the digest option (see above) should help you do this.

- Be careful with using the reply button: do not embarrass yourself or your charity by sending personal, private or internal information to the list by mistake. Whereas a wrongly-addressed letter is received by only one person or one organisation, on the lists hundreds of people get to see the mistake.

- Even though e-mail offers a near instant response, re-read what you have typed and do not send it off immediately. It is tempting to adopt an informal tone but remember your e-mail messages on behalf of your charity should be as professional and correctly-spelled as your letters on paper.

- Use clear subject headings to help others decide at a glance whether your message is relevant to them.

- Cross-posting, or sending the same message to more than one list, is usually acceptable but should be done in moderation as it can annoy those who are subscribed to several lists to come across your message again and again.

What fundraisers gain from discussion lists

Various studies of the North American fundraising discussion lists have shed light on what fundraisers feel they gain from the discussion lists. These benefits include:

- gaining a rapid education by networking with other fundraisers
- sounding out ideas with more experienced fundraisers before learning the hard way
- making contact with other fundraisers, particularly valuable to the solo fundraiser working in isolation

A number of studies of the fundraising lists have revealed interesting aspects of their nature. According to a 1995 survey, FUNDLIST was a widely-used resource, it was not the preserve of a few dominant contributors, and it took contributions from nearly one third of its 1,650 subscribers over a seven-week period. Another survey found that FUNDLIST was "a kinder, gentler list than some, even in some other professional and academic circles", and that its subscribers were "a practical, as opposed to philosophical group". The friendly tone of FUNDLIST was welcoming to the constant flow of newcomers who joined the list, some of them new not just to the list but to online communications as a whole.

Where on earth else?

The lists have been particularly useful for some of the more unusual problems fundraisers encounter from time to time. Some would have found great difficulty in finding an answer to their questions elsewhere. Some of the more outlandish questions that have been posed to the lists have come from the fundraiser wishing to sell $600,000 worth of donated timber without selling the land on which it was growing, the fundraiser who had to fix a tax-deductible amount to a donated cadaver, and the fundraiser who had to work out the tax-deductible value of a racehorse. The fundraiser with the trickiest problem, however, must have been the one who had to deal with a woman who wanted to leave $3 million in stocks and bonds but who would be "reanimated" after being frozen at death and would then reclaim all her money. She wanted this in writing because of course the fundraiser was not going to be alive when she returned!

Fundraising newsgroups

Newsgroups are similar discussion fora to e-mail discussion lists but are to be found on Usenet, the worldwide discussion network that hosts thousands of newsgroups on a variety of different subjects. An e-mail list and a newsgroup could contain exactly the same messages but in general the difference is that messages from an e-mail list will be delivered to your desktop computer, whereas you will have to make an effort to visit a newsgroup. Similarly, to receive an e-mail list's messages you have to subscribe to the list whereas you can visit a newsgroup without joining it in any formal sense.

There are no newsgroups that concentrate solely on fundraising. There are, however, several that cover nonprofit issues. One of these, soc.org.nonprofit, is particularly useful to fundraisers. In the hierarchical naming convention that is behind the Usenet system, soc.org.nonprofit translates roughly as "discussions on society, in particular organisations that are nonprofit in nature". Apart from daily discussions that frequently cover fundraising, those who frequent the newsgroup have created a Frequently Asked Questions (or FAQ) as a reference guide for participants. The soc.org.nonprofit FAQ is one of the finest free resources available to charity professionals and fundraisers on the Internet. It is broken down into sections like a well-ordered book and is effectively the sum knowledge of the newsgroup's participants, distilled and offered free of charge. You can access it from Putnam Barber's home page at <http://www.eskimo.com/pbarber>. Actually, soc.org.nonprofit is the newsgroup version of the Usnonprofit-l list, so you can choose how you access the information. No other fundraising or charity lists, however, exist in both newsgroup and e-mail list format.

Accessing Usenet newsgroups requires specific "newsreader" software, but this is usually included with any Internet connection purchased now. Also World Wide Web browsers such as Netscape Navigator are now increasingly incorporating access to Usenet newsgroups as one of their standard functions.

For more information on e-mail lists and newsgroups

Finding out which lists and newsgroups are available is covered in Chapter 13. For more detailed information on using the various types of e-mail list try James Milles' *Discussion Lists: Mail Server Commands*. This guide is available free of charge by sending the message:
GET MAILSER CMD NETTRAIN F=MAIL
to e-mail address: listserv@ubvm.cc.buffalo.edu

Summary

- You can use e-mail to seek free advice from thousands of other fundraisers from around the world at any time of the day.

- There is a growing number of focused e-mail discussion lists on different aspects of fundraising.

- Subscribing to lists is free.

- Use the lists to ask questions, share your experience, discuss issues, learn about new information resources, and receive job vacancy announcements.

- Using e-mail lists can be time-consuming and offer pitfalls for the unwary - think before you post!

- When you find out how useful e-mail lists are to you, think of how useful they could be for communicating with your charity's donors.

5 WHO IS OUT THERE? INTERNET DEMOGRAPHICS

The Internet offers a variety of methods of communicating with potential donors, but are the donors online to hear fundraisers' messages? Is there an online audience worth targeting?

Accurate and consistent statistics for the demographic details of Internet users have been notoriously difficult to obtain. Even the number of people with access to the Internet has been a matter of heated debate, with estimates ranging from a few million to 60 million. To confuse matters further, "access to the Internet" covers a range of activity from the occasional use of the e-mail system at work to the home PC user who explores the Internet for an hour or so every evening.

It is certain that there are very many individuals using the Internet. Home computing and membership of consumer online services such as CompuServe and America Online have both been areas of considerable and rapid growth over the last few years. The UK, for example, now has the highest level of personal computer ownership in the world, with one third of households owning a personal computer. It is reasonable to suppose that these many Internet users include current donors to charities. In fact, we know this is true because in the USA donors themselves have established e-mail and WWW resources to discuss their charitable giving, such as the GIVING list (see Chapter 6). Those Internet users who are not currently donors to charity are also worth investigating as potential donors. Fundraisers should expect their Internet fundraising to include both donor cultivation and donor prospecting.

Fortunately for fundraisers, the quality, frequency and coverage of surveys of Internet users has improved considerably over the last couple of years. Even if the question of quantity is put to one side, much more is now being found out about the quality of Internet users in terms of their income, gender and age. US statistics are certainly easier to come by but UK statistics are available, too. In both cases however the old stereotype of Internet users as US teenage male students is no longer applicable.

A valuable target market

Many surveys confirm that Internet users are often well-educated and have household incomes that are notably higher than average. Even the 1995 survey by Trish Information Services for O'Reilly & Associates that reported only 5.8 million Internet users, in addition to the 3.9 million estimated commercial online service users, reported that the median household income of such users was in the $50,000 to $75,000 range.

Previously the Second GVU WWW User Survey (one of the oldest and largest demographic surveys of Internet users) in October and November 1994 had reported that 43% of respondents had incomes between $35,000 and $75,000, <**http://www.cc.gatech.edu/gvu/user_surveys/survey-09-1994/**>.

A similarly consistent result of many surveys is that the percentage of women users of the Internet is growing. A survey of North American Internet users in 1995 found that about one-third of users of the Internet were women and that the trend suggested an even male/female ratio some time early in 1997.

The average age of Internet users is increasing. The mean age for the Third GVU WWW User Survey in mid-1995 was 35 years, up from 31 in the Second Survey conducted just six months before. The average age for men and women users is almost the same. The Internet is not the preserve of the young: older people are using it as well. A survey in 1994 found 4.6% of respondents aged 50-55 and 2.2% over 55. These figures are confirmed by the number of resources being produced on the Internet for and by older people. A bimonthly WWW newsletter for those over 50 was launched in August 1995 and in November that year a WWW site for older women "Women at Midlife" was created to offer "a support forum for older women" together with a newsletter.

UK Internet users

Far less information is available on the demographics of UK Internet users compared with the USA but there are figures available. The UK's first nation-wide surveys of users of the Internet in the UK were carried out by the National Opinion Poll's Research Group between March and April 1995, and they produced some of the first UK-specific figures that marketers and fundraisers could use reliably. <http://www.maires.co.uk/inet.html> The surveys showed that 2.35 million people in the UK had used the Internet in the past year and most of them (65%) were aged 25-55 with high disposable incomes. Thirty five percent of them earned over £25,000 a year, and a quarter of users travelled abroad on business. Almost one third of users were female, and 6% of users were aged 55 or more. The total number of users was growing at a rate of 10% per month.

Lessons for fundraisers

The US and UK surveys demonstrate that those who use the Internet should be regarded as good prospects. Internet users are a valuable audience to fundraisers both in terms of prospecting for new high-income donors and developing new forms of online relationships with existing donors who use the Internet. Internet users are wealthier, include men and women (the ratio between which is getting closer to parity over time), and comprise a wide age range which includes older people. The percentage of users aged 55 is particularly interesting, given the value fundraisers place on securing legacy donations from donors. The concept of relationship fundraising applies just as much to fundraising online as it does offline: a single WWW page directed at an under-30s audience, providing options for giving that are relevant to them, such as payroll giving and credit card donations, might not prove relevant to older visitors. Only a few charities have spotted the growing number of older Internet users: Greenpeace and Cambridge University both announced plans to provide a legacy information page on their WWW sites in September 1995.

The fact that the NOP survey found that 20% of UK Internet users did not read a daily newspaper is also significant. It suggests that the Internet can help fundraisers reach a new market which was previously unavailable via traditional print advertising appeals.

Surveying your donors' use of the Internet

Of course, direct marketing fundraisers will still require far more detailed information before they feel they understand the online market sufficiently, but such information is available from the market research companies, at a price of course. All the information presented here is publicly available free of charge. Information on Internet users is also being built up by the national consumer survey organisations, many of which are now asking if householders own a PC and access the Internet.

Whilst this information should make it clear that the Internet is used by many individuals to whom fundraisers might very well wish to appeal, in practice fundraisers are never going to be interested in every one of the thirty, forty, or sixty million users that apparently populate the Internet. Fundraisers will concentrate on addressing two key audiences, their prospective donors on the Internet and, equally importantly, their existing donors who use the Internet.

Fortunately, producing statistical information on these two target audiences is simply a matter of asking for it. A key component of planning an Internet fundraising strategy is researching the number of existing donors or supporters who already use the Internet. If a charity already has a number of donors using the Internet then they can find out if such donors would like to receive information or other services on the Internet, either via e-mail or the World Wide Web. Asking donors what they want is, of course, central to good fundraising practice, but how many charities when setting up their World Wide Web sites ask their donors what they would like to find on them? They certainly announce them in their membership and donor newsletters but almost always as a one-way service the charity gives to their supporters. This is not a failing of charities alone. Anecdotal evidence from a recent study suggested that 90% of corporations had created their Web sites without consulting their clients and customers about what they wanted from them.

Once a charity knows the views and level of experience with the Internet of its existing donors it can then find out more about those donors who were recruited via the Internet. It is quite possible, for example, that the profile of donors recruited via the Internet will be different from your charity's existing donor profile. As soon as a charity creates a World Wide Web site it should include prominently a survey form to enable more to be learnt about the type of Internet users visiting the site. Forms can also be sent to donors by e-mail. These surveys should give fundraisers information not only about those who give online, but also about those who had visited the site but had not chosen to give. There is nothing wrong with asking why someone chose not to give. It might be a technical matter such as concern over the security of personal information transmitted over the Internet, or because the charity had presented visitors with too little or too much information. Whatever the barrier to giving, fundraisers need to know what it is in order to remove it.

Form-filling on the Internet is not the chore that it is with paper questionnaires, not least because you do not have to find a pen and an envelope. Provided the questionnaire is well-designed, visitors often jump at the chance to provide feedback, particularly if there is little else on the Web page for them to interact with. Of course, statistics from such surveys are open to interpretation in that respondents are self-selected. Nevertheless, fundraisers can use them to adapt their site to reflect and serve its visitors' needs better. The key to success in using these statistics is to gather them on a regular basis. Your chariety's World Wide Web site and other Internet-based activities will not remain static: as they expand and develop so you need to keep track of the donors and supporters they are attracting and recruiting.

Further information

Those charities that cannot afford to purchase the often expensive market research reports but still wish to keep up with general Internet demographic figures can visit:

O'Reilly & Associates' Internet Market Research
<http://www.ora.com/www/info/research/index.html>

FIND/SVP, a worldwide research and consulting firm
<http://etrg.findsvp.com>

A selection of the major Internet surveys provided by Nua
<http://www.nua.ie/Choice/Surveys/SurveyLinks.html>

Graphics, Visualization, & Usability (GVU) Center's World Wide Web User
Surveys at <http://www.cc.gatech.edu/gvu/user_surveys/>

Summary

- The quality, frequency and coverage of market research surveys of Internet users has improved considerably.

- Ignore the debate about the numbers of people using the Internet; it is the quality of users that should interest fundraisers.

- Internet users are often wealthier and better educated than average.

- The proportion of female to male users is getting closer to parity.

- Over-55's use the Internet as well as younger people.

- Find out how many of your charity's existing supporters and donors, both individual and corporate, already use the Internet.

- Ask visitors to your charity's World Wide Web site, using a survey form, why they gave and why some of them do not.

- Repeat the surveys regularly.

- Look at other charities' online questionnaires; what information are they asking for?

- Do the donors you attract via the Internet match your existing donor profile?

6 DONORS ON THE INTERNET

The profiles of the type of people who use the Internet should already sound promising to fundraisers. If anyone needed convincing that individual donors are online they should join the GIVING e-mail discussion list. This is a list set up to enable donors and potential donors to compare and contrast charities to determine which might be best suited or most worthy of their gift.

You can join the GIVING e-mail list by sending the message:
Subscribe giving Firstname Lastname
to e-mail address: listproc@envirolink.org

The list's creator has also established the Internet NonProfit Center <**http://www.human.com:80/inc/**> to help donors to decide where to direct their charitable gifts. Cliff Landesman wanted to make it "faster, cheaper, and easier" for donors to learn about charities. The Center runs a "Best Buys for Big Hearts" list of top charities in various categories, as ranked by the American Institute of Philanthropy with its figures for the percentage of a charity's income spent on charitable activity. The site also contains details of the Center's "Donor's Defense Kit" which suggests how to say "No" without guilt to fundraisers' appeals and how to get hold of more information on charities. It is encouraging to see an independent donor-centric resource such as the Internet NonProfit Center: fundraisers would do well to visit it to see the real concerns and requirements of donors.

As well as the Internet NonProfit Center, US donors can also consult Benefice to assist them in their charitable giving. Launched in Summer 1995, it is available in CD-ROM format, on the WWW and on a major commercial online service, Benefice helps potential donors make informed decisions in their charitable giving. Users can pinpoint the suitable beneficiary by searching by organisation name and area of funding interest. They can then use the financial, geographical and governing board information presented, together with videos by certain charities.

The UK has similar resources, although not directed solely at assisting the potential donor. The Charities Aid Foundation's WWW site <**http://www.charitynet.org**> includes information on the organisation's services to donors to assist and advise them on the best methods of donating to charity.

Hemmington Scott Publishing Ltd <**http://www.hemscott.co.uk/hemscott**>, publishers of *The Henderson Top 2000 Charities*, offers free information on the top 5000 UK charities at its CharitiesDirect WWW site <**http://www.world-**

server.pipex.com/hemscott/chardir/index.htm>. Entries for charities include five year income and expenditure figures, contact details, policy statements, and the names of trustees and executive staff. It also provides information on the professional advisers to charities with listings of their current clients. Information on corporate donors and their charitable expenditure is also available. The information is searchable via indices of charity name, size, expenditure classification and geographical region.

Aurelian Information, publishers of *Who's Who In The Voluntary Sector,* have created a number of database information sources on the UK voluntary sector, including listings by subject, personnel, type and income of the 7000+ most important charities and voluntary organisations in the UK national sector. Their on-line searchable database is available to subscribers using an off-line reader for high speed and very detailed search and sort operations. Information on *Charities-On-Line* and Aurelian's other products is available at **<http:///www.dircon.co.uk/aurelian>**.

Grant-makers online

As well as individual donors on the Internet, there is a considerable amount of information on grant-making bodies available online, from private through corporate to statutory bodies. Some of this information is held in online directories by commercial publishers or by umbrella organisations for grant-makers but many grant-making bodies publish the information online themselves.

A growing number of trusts and foundations have online presences. Indeed the US Council on Foundations' conference in May 1995 was told *"all grant makers have a growing responsibility to learn about new technologies, to start using them, and to help charities think about ways in which technology can help streamline their work".* US foundations with online presences include:

Carnegie Foundation	**<http://www.ezweb.com:80/carnegie/>**
J Paul Getty Trust	**<http://www.ahip.getty.edu/ahip/Text_trust.html>**
John Simon Guggenheim Foundation	**<http://gf.org>**
Rockefeller Brothers Fund	**<http://www.rbf.org/rbf/>**

One US foundation, the John D and Catherine T MacArthur Foundation, launched a gopher site in early 1995 carrying details of grant recipients in the previous year and the size of grants they received. The Foundation also published guidance on how to make a grant application, together with background information on the Foundation, its board and staff members. The Foundation has subsequently launched a World Wide Web site **<http://www.macfdn.org>**. Certainly all this information was already available in paper form but publication on the Internet of information on trusts and foundations offers great benefits to fundraisers:

- the information on the trust is (or should be) current
- the information is available on demand ie no delay due to postal delivery
- the information is searchable. Internet search engines (see Chapter 13) can now help fundraisers locate information on specific trusts, areas of support, and even imminent grant deadlines.

At the same time, far from all trusts and foundations have an Internet presence themselves so a search of the Internet will not provide a comprehensive solution. UK grant-making trusts for example have been very slow in developing online presences. The existing trust and foundation directories, whether on paper or CD-ROM, will continue to be essential for coverage, at least until these directories are made available online too.

Some grant-makers, although they do not have WWW sites, still provide information by e-mail. For example the CS Fund in the US provides its current annual brochure, containing information on applying for a grant and a list of the foundation's grants last year, via an automatic-reply e-mailer or "autobot" (see Chapter 7). To receive a copy send an e-mail to: csfund-brochure@igc.apc.org. Searching for trusts and foundations solely on the WWW will therefore not produce a comprehensive result; e-mail address search engines should also be used (see Chapter 13).

Umbrella organisations for grant-making foundations have also established Internet presences which provide useful information for both member foundations and grant-seeking fundraisers. The National Council on Foundations in the US, with over 1,300 members, has a WWW page **<http://www.cof.org>** with a directory of Regional Associations of Grant-makers, as well as links to other foundations' WWW pages. The Foundation Center's WWW page **<http://fdncenter.org>**, launched in January 1995, contains a variety of practical information including details on its hardcopy publications, brief tips on how to research foundations, addresses for its regional research libraries, and links to other foundations' WWW pages. It also archives copies of *The Philanthropy Review* **<http://fdncenter.org/phil/philmain.html>**.

Corporate supporters online

Some of the foundations with Internet presences and activities are the charitable giving arms of for-profit companies. Certainly many companies include information on their WWW sites on their corporate trust's charitable giving activities. Apple and Sun Microsystems both include such information.

Corporate giving, of course, is not limited to charitable donations via a trust or foundation. Some charities' WWW pages contain evidence of corporate support in a variety of ways. Some include the logo of a corporate sponsor. Others acknowledge the practical support of staff on secondment. Yet more feature news of fundraising events involving company staff. In other words, for-profit companies, the number of which registering their .com domain names increased by 61% in the first quarter of 1996 alone, include those of charitable intent. (This increase does not, for example, include those companies in the UK registering as .co.uk). As with private foundations, fundraisers can search the Internet for such organisations' charitable giving policy or examples of such charitable support. They can also check to see if their existing corporate supporters have an online presence, and perhaps arrange further support for the charity's online activities. In the UK, the Charities Aid Foundation <http://www.charitynet.org/> provides a list of links to the pages of over 70 UK companies detailing their charitable support.

Statutory funding sources

Government funding information is increasingly available on the Internet. The US federal government has published extensive details of its funding programmes on the WWW. The European Union has also established WWW sites with details on the various grants available to charities and businesses <http://www.echo.lu>.

The UK Government's site at <http://www.open.gov.uk> includes information on various bodies which provide funding. It is also possible to view the full list of charity recipients of the National Lottery Charities Board grants <http://www.aslib.co.uk/lottery/index.html>.

Summary

- The Internet is populated by a multitude of donors of interest to fundraisers in organisations large and small.

- Donors on the Internet include individual donors, corporate donors, foundations and government bodies.

- Some of these donors you will wish to provide information to, others you will seek to receive information from.

- Extensive information on these donors is freely available on the Internet, from demographic details on Internet users through grant-making policies of foundations to the full-text of European-wide funding schemes.

7 FUNDRAISING APPEALS BY E-MAIL

E-mail alone can be one of the most effective online fundraising tools. At its heart is a direct communication from one person to another. Yet e-mail is often overlooked by fundraisers in the rush to acquire a WWW site.

Electronic mail remains the lingua franca of the Internet. It is the basic form of communication that underpins the Internet and as such is the one sure method of making contact with other people online. While debate rages about the number of people who have access to the World Wide Web and even more debate rages about the number of people who actually make use of this access, everyone with access to the Internet must by definition have an e-mail facility. In fact, despite the time and money invested in WWW sites, it is quite possible that the most successful fundraising conducted on the Internet will be carried out via e-mail. Full WWW access (including the ability to use graphics, sound and video) assumes a fairly advanced national telecommunications system, which of course the majority of countries around the world do not possess. Even in countries that do have such systems, not everyone who uses a computer uses an up-to-date model that can cope with graphics. So it makes sense to base one's Internet fundraising strategy at the basic, lowest common denominator level of e-mail.

E-mail appeals: pros and cons

Using e-mail must form the cornerstone of a fundraiser's strategy for fundraising on the Internet. Above all it is cheap and fast and, unlike a World Wide Web site, necessarily targeted to a known individual via their e-mail address. World Wide Web sites might be more visually compelling than the text-only impact of an e-mail message, but they are often used as little more than a generic online brochure. Web sites can be used much more effectively, as explained in Chapter 10, but they will not provide the personal, direct mail-type impact that an e-mail message achieves.

However, in discussions on the fundraising discussion lists many North American fundraisers voiced their belief that e-mail appeals, or electronic direct mail, could not work. The spectre of the junk e-mail appeal arose. Some argued that e-mail appeals could not work because they were too intrusive, not every donor could be reached because they did not all have computers and e-mail addresses, and appeals did not suit the medium of e-mail where messages tended to be short and where upfront sales messages contravened the concept of "netiquette". Fundraisers who have successfully integrated telemarketing, or fundraising using the telephone, might recognise these objections as similar to those that were voiced when the idea of actually speaking to donors via the telephone was first raised.

Fundraising appeals via e-mail have been employed for a number of years, and the various methods available are discussed below. However, the above objections need to be addressed if the fundraiser is to secure organisation-wide approval to proceed with this type of fundraising.

Junk mail has been described as bad direct mail. Junk e-mail then can be similarly rejected as poorly targeted e-mail. It will no doubt continue to be sent and received but any charity that adopts the scattergun approach to marketing is wasting its resources and is likely to harm its public reputation. Certainly, junk e-mail is much easier and cheaper to distribute than paper junk mail, but such cost savings are of little relevance if, as a fundraiser, you are aiming to friend-raise as well as fundraise. The fact that you can annoy many more times the number of prospective donors for a fraction of the cost of a printed direct-mail appeal should be of no interest to the professional fundraiser.

This scattergun approach is sadly common on the Internet and is known as 'spamming'. In particular this term describes the often indiscriminate posting of the same message, usually a sales pitch, to dozens and even hundreds of e-mail lists and newsgroups, irrespective of their discussion subject. Any charity attempting such an approach will be remembered for quite a while by many people!

So it is true that mass appeals to millions of Internet users should not be conducted by e-mail, if, of course, a fundraiser ever thought that such a loudhailer approach was ever likely to work. But that does not stop e-mail appeals being sent to people who have asked to receive them. These could include existing donors who prefer to receive appeals or membership subscription reminders by e-mail, or visitors to a charity's World Wide Web site who ask to receive further information. These are the effective e-mail appeals, as will be seen from the examples below.

Consent is therefore the key to running e-mail appeals, which should come as no surprise to those committed to relationship fundraising (see Chapter 12). Apart from complying with data protection legislation on holding personal data (such as e-mail addresses) in electronic form, such a relationship approach should remove the objection that e-mail appeals are intrusive.

Of course, not all donors have access to computers and nor are they likely to, so e-mail appeals are not going to replace the more comprehensive direct mail fundraising approaches of charities. But then few charities contact all their donors by telephone. They will choose a selection and will tailor their fundraising message to them. So, too, is the case with e-mail appeals. Fundraisers will be contacting a specific constituency within their donor base with a particular message.

As for e-mail being suitable only for succinct messages, even if this were true, then it would be a matter of developing a suitable copywriting style that fits the medium. Perhaps the standard three- or four-page direct mail appeal will have to be condensed to the equivalent of a single page for an e-mail appeal, but this will only be determined by repeated testing - the direct-mail fundraiser's watchword.

Elements of an e-mail fundraising campaign

SIGNATURES

The simplest general fundraising appeal is the one-line request that is included in your e-mail signature. E-mail signatures are the equivalent of letterheads and usually include your full name, organisation's name, e-mail address, postal address and telephone and fax number. Most e-mail packages can be customised to append automatically such details to every message you send. Some people include a quotation or proverb underneath this, often as a way of personalising the message. A charity can, instead, include a request for funds, either as a general appeal or for a particular project that needs funding. The emphasis is on short and powerful messages. Include a donation telephone hotline number if you have one, or your PO Box number. Do not forget to code the appeal so that you can track its effectiveness; for example, ask for donations to be posted to Room XYZ.

Your e-mail signature will then be seen by everyone to whom you send an e-mail - donors, local groups, enquirers, suppliers, journalists, trustees and colleagues. It is an unobtrusive reminder that your charity needs financial support. Those fundraisers working in larger charities should try to create a standard signature incorporating this one- or two-line appeal for everyone in the organisation.

Some real examples of fundraising e-mail "sigs":

"Donations gratefully accepted and desperately needed at Children's Legal Center"

"a leading UK AIDS fundraising charity... please consider making a donation to CRUSAID as part of your visit to the ArtAIDS galleries"

E-MAIL FORMS

As almost all donations require a form to be filled in, fundraisers should convert their standard donation form to an e-mail file to send in response to an enquiry. The form probably already exists in word-processed format so can easily be converted for use in an e-mail message, thereby removing the need to type in the whole form each time. (This usually involves reducing the width of the text to about 80 characters to ensure it can be read on any type of computer screen that the recipient has, and saving the file in ASCII format).

The donor can then complete the e-mail form on-screen and send it back, or they can print it out and post it or fax it. The latter is the only option for documents such as deeds of covenant that legally require a signature. Those donors concerned about security of credit card numbers sent by e-mail (see Chapter 14) might also prefer to fax or post a completed credit card donation form.

AUTO-RESPONDERS

When fundraisers clock off at the end of the day they cannot respond to requests for information on how to donate. Fortunately, e-mail can be customised to allow a 24-hour response, working while the fundraiser sleeps and helping to reduce the workload during the day.

Auto-responders, also known as mailbots or infobots, are software packages that allow a file to be sent automatically in response to an e-mail message received. An enquirer sends an e-mail message, often without any subject or text in the body of the message, to the auto-responder's address and a file is e-mailed back to them straight away. This file can contain anything, but a fundraiser might include a list of all the different methods of making a donation, perhaps in the style of a form. Auto-responder messages can afford to be more detailed than other types of e-mail appeals as the would-be donor has specifically requested the information.

If a general auto-responder proves successful further responders can be added. Instead of the general address such as help@charityname.org, a charity could have a range such as

covenant@charityname.org
trading@charityname.org
creditcard@charityname.org
companygift@charityname.org

Auto-responder software usually includes an automatic tracking system so that a fundraiser can receive or access regular statistics on the number of people who have requested such information. Automatically supplied with the name and e-mail address of each enquirer, they can then conduct a follow-up campaign to those whose enquiry did not result in a donation.

As with other fundraising activities, the auto-responder can be used to "test, test and test again". A series of different auto-responder addresses can be used, perhaps as part of a segmented direct mail appeal or in a variety of newspaper advertisements: some donors will, for example, be asked to respond to thank-you1@charityname.org, and others will be asked to e-mail their pledge to thank-you2@charityname.org. The impact of each appeal can then be determined from the number and total value of responses sent to each auto-responder address. In other words auto-responders can be incorporated to assist in evaluating other more 'traditional' fundraising appeals.

Amnesty International USA began offering a simple donation and membership form by auto-responder in 1994. The message returned encouraged the enquirer to "Become a member of Amnesty International by making a tax-deductible donation". The form also offered information on how else to get involved and a brief advertisement for an Amnesty International CD-ROM product. Recipients were encouraged to print out the form, complete it and return it by mail rather than by e-mail.

Friends of the Earth run an automated information server. A message to info@foe.co.uk will produce a reply introducing FoE, explaining why it is now time to act, what FoE has already achieved and what your support can do. It concludes by asking the recipient to join as a member. As well as a donation and membership form, the e-mail includes a monthly standing order form.

ADVANCED USES OF AUTO-RESPONDERS
Auto-responders offer more than the simple donation-form-on-request service. Instead of a straight-forward text file an interactive set of forms can be returned. These "presentations" are small software packages that can be saved to the enquirer's PC and then run like any other software, irrespective of the software packages they already have. An example of such a presentation can be retrieved free of charge by sending a message (there is no need to write anything in the message) to interactive@reply.net. ReplyNet is a US company that offers a variety of marketing-by-e-mail services.

The security features of auto-responder software allow fundraisers to restrict access to particular donors or would-be donors who have been issued with a password. Thus a major gift donors club could be issued with privileged information ahead of other donors or supporters, or perhaps with an invitation to the charity's gala evening. On a larger scale, charities with membership schemes could offer their newsletter to members only. Money-off coupons can be offered, perhaps to promote the charity's merchandise.

It is possible both to block enquiries from particular e-mail addresses, whole organisations or even whole countries and, conversely, to serve requests for information only if the enquirer's e-mail address is included on a set of pre-defined privileged addresses. In other words, the fundraiser can control who gets to access the information.

Online surveys can also be automated using an auto-responder. This might prove a useful method of finding out for the first time which donors are online. Existing donors are contacted via direct mail or the charity newsletter and asked to submit their details (name, address, e-mail address etc) via the online survey. Instead of dealing with each message himself, the fundraiser will have the details of at least some of the charity's online donors in electronic format, which can be checked against the charity's existing donor database.

E-mail appeals

It should be clear that mass e-mail appeals are unlikely to succeed and should not be attempted. However a number of charities have used small-scale appeals by e-mail and have enjoyed some success. A model example is the fundraising of Plugged In, a US nonprofit that introduces disadvantaged children to information technology. The nonprofit has run a series of short but well-written e-mail appeals to potential donors and purchasers of their services in order to raise funds <http://www.impactonline.org/words/internet/plugged.html>.

In addition to contacting local business people with this e-mail they now ask their volunteers to forward a standard e-mail appeal and to post it appropriately on bulletin boards and mailing lists. The message evidently proves successful for the organisation. One factor in its success must be the e-mail message's announcement at the beginning of the text that this is a fundraising appeal, combined with its polite offer of a valuable service, concluding with information on how to receive further information and how to avoid it.

Direct Marketing via e-mail?

Appeals via e-mail might well generate more income than appeals on WWW sites but they will not take the place of traditional direct mail appeals for four reasons.

44

- Despite increasing numbers of people and organisations acquiring PCs at home and at work, it is highly unlikely that every donor and every prospective donor will ever have an e-mail address, whereas they are much more likely to have a physical address.

- Those donors who do have e-mail addresses are likely to change them more often than they move house. Companies providing Internet access, and therefore e-mail addresses, will come and go, taking their yourname@theircompany.name.com address with them when they cease trading. Similarly donors will switch allegiances and move their accounts to other Internet service providers, and will therefore have to change their addresses. Those using their company's e-mail account will lose access when they move jobs. Certainly, there are ways of acquiring a portable e-mail address but not everyone will do so. So the online databases of e-mail addresses that are freely available and searchable (see Chapter 13), even if they were comprehensive and up-to-date (which they are unlikely to be) will be out of date faster than the databases of individuals' physical addresses.

- Those that do have e-mail addresses might well have more than one such address. The author had two e-mail addresses at his university, one which was checked every day and the other only once or twice a month. At the same time he had two separate e-mail addresses at work, and another for his Internet connection at home. A charity's urgent appeal to the the "wrong" e-mail address would have elicited a very slow response, yet the author used e-mail every day. That might be an extreme case but it should not be forgotten that having two e-mail addresses is not uncommon.

- E-mail addresses cannot be used to profile a charity's donorbase in the same way that physical addresses can. A postcode can be used to infer a variety of lifestyle attributes to a donor but an e-mail address can not. An e-mail address is in many ways placeless. Domain names can sometimes reveal if the message comes from an individual or organisation, what type of organisation it is, and from which country the message was sent, but in many cases this can not be guaranteed. For example, an e-mail can be sent with a .uk address by someone who happens to be accessing his e-mail account in the USA. Similarly a message from a .com address need not be sent officially; it could be an employee misusing the company's e-mail account to send a personal message.

There is no sign yet of reciprocal e-mail mailings between charities whereby they swap the e-mail addresses of an agreed number of their respective supporters and donors. The above reasons would suggest this would be an unlikely development but it might be feasible, if the lists were used within days rather than weeks.

There are indications that marketing via e-mail is being accorded the same value as traditional direct marketing. There is now even a Direct Electronic Mail Marketing Association **<http://www.memo.net/demma/dema.html>** through which people can ask not to receive e-mail from companies, much like the UK's Mailing Preference Service. This initiative is encouraging if it leads to a reduction in the amount of junk e-mail.

In general however, e-mail addresses will probably be used in conjunction with existing demographic data based on donors' physical address details and not alone. An online appeal that ignores this information might still work but the fundraiser will not be able to draw many practical marketing conclusions from the results.

And finally..

Another reason to concentrate one's Internet fundraising strategy at the level of e-mail is that, for many people, e-mail is their only way of accessing any aspect of the Internet. E-mail is even more valuable than many people imagine. Using e-mail alone it is possible to access almost all the aspects of the Internet, from World Wide Web through Archie, FTP, gopher and Veronica, to WAIS. This is good news for those without access to the necessary software or services. For further details get hold of a (free) copy of *Accessing The Internet By E-Mail* Doctor Bob's Guide to Offline Internet Access by sending the relevant message to one of the addresses below:

For those in UK, Europe and Asia:
Message: send lis-iis e-access-inet.txt
to e-mail address: mailbase@mailbase.ac.uk

For those in the USA and Canada:
Message: GET INTERNET BY-EMAIL NETTRAIN F=MAIL
to e-mail address: listserv@ubvm.cc.buffalo.edu

Summary

- E-mail, not the World Wide Web, is the basic form of communication that underpins the Internet and is therefore the one sure method of making contact with other people online.

- Despite the attraction of the World Wide Web the most successful fundraising conducted on the Internet will be carried out via e-mail.

- Junk e-mail is even easier to send than junk direct mail, but just because you can e-mail millions of people does not mean that you should.

- E-mail appeals should be targeted, sent to consenting recipients, be more concise than direct mail appeals, and include some kind of response mechanism... which should not sound too revolutionary.

- Incorporate a fundraising message in the signature at the bottom of every e-mail message you send, and preferably every e-mail message your charity sends.

- Convert your donation form to a text format that can be sent by e-mail, for completion and return by e-mail, or for printing out and return by fax or post.

- Offer a 24-hour automatic response to would-be donors using an auto-responder.

- E-mail appeals will not replace traditional direct mail appeals.

8 APPEALS ON THE INTERNET: THE WORLD WIDE WEB

It took nearly three weeks for the press to locate and publish complete infor-mation about which organizations were doing what in Rwanda. It was clear that a faster infrastructure for global relief could have helped... We realized that the Internet provides just such an infrastructure - both social and techno-logical.

Nova Spivack, Earthweb and Reliefnet, WEBster, September 1994

The World Wide Web, with its ability to display text, graphics and even video and sound on a page, together with its point-and-click user-friendly navigation system, is now almost synonymous with the Internet. If one is asked "are you on the Internet?", the questioner often means "do you use the World Wide Web?" and perhaps even "have you got a World Wide Web page?".

Certainly the World Wide Web has been embraced by many commercial organisations eager to exploit a major new communications medium with a global reach. So, too, many charities have correctly identified it as a flexible tool through which they can extend and amplify some or even all of their current fundraising activities. This excitement is understandable given the successful innovations by a number of charities on their World Wide Web pages, and the vast possibilities awaiting those that realise how to create and maintain successful fundraising pages.

Creating an appeal with a donation form on a Web page is a fundamental and essential component of using the Internet to raise funds. It can require little extra work as you will probably simply use the text and graphics of your existing fundraising brochure and donation form. As long as it does not become out of date it can remain on your Web site for as long as you want, 24 hours a day. As most accounts with Internet Service Providers now include a free 0.5 Mb of Web space it would be foolish not to at least create a basic page to allow visitors to your charity's Web site the opportunity to respond with a donation. Although, as explained in Chapter 7, e-mail is likely to be a more effective fundraising tool, a permanently-available Web page can certainly help to increase the number of donors and supporters recruited through a charity's Internet presence.

In practice, there are more issues to consider. In Chapter 2, for example, it was recommended that a charity should not create a fundraising page only but instead publish information on all aspects of the charity's work on an integrated Web site. Issues such as who maintains the fundraising Web page information, how it is combined with existing fundraising activity, and using the Web for a variety of fundraising activities are covered in Chapters 9 to 12.

Gopher appeals

A number of charities have created static online fundraising appeals for several years, some of them using a forerunner of the World Wide Web, the Internet information distribution system gopher.

Gopher is a menu-based system of storing and retrieving information in files and directories. To retrieve information you scroll up and down a hierarchical list of menus until you reach the directory you are seeking. More significantly, gopher is a text-based system: there can be no graphics displayed on a text file that is viewable by gopher. Yet this did not stop a few pioneering fundraisers from trying out appeals on their organisations' gopher servers.

Griefnet, for example, an online resource on bereavement and loss, included fundraising appeals on its top gopher menu:

```
Home Gopher server: gopher.rivendell.org

1. About Griefnet
2. What's New?
3. Frequently Asked Questions
4. Bereavement and Loss Resources Directory/
5. Professional Resources Directory/
6. Annotated Bibliography of Grief & Loss Media
7. About the Association for Death Education and
   Counselling/
8. About Rivendell Resources
9. Contributions to Griefnet
10. Supporters of Griefnet
```

Similarly the British Library included its 'Adopt a Book Appeal' on its gopher site in June 1994, see overleaf. Although a static and visually unappealing page (the text appears in Courier typeface), it nevertheless demonstrates some foresight on the part of the National Preservation Office of the British Library. Unfortunately the appeal did not generate any income in the first 18 months. **<gopher://portico.bl.uk/00/portico/services/preserv/adopt.txt>**.

A fundraising appeal on a gopher page, however, is certainly going to have less impact than an e-mail message. At least an e-mail message is sent to a recipient, whereas a file on a gopher server has to be accessed by choice. This is the same as a fundraising appeal on a World Wide Web page. Unless you can make it compelling, and give donors a reason for accessing the file, it is a very static fundraising device, the online equivalent of a charity collecting tin on a shop counter.

Webbed feats: World Wide Web appeals

The interactive graphical capabilities of WWW pages have been used to good effect by a number of charities in a variety of ways. Mostly, though, fundraisers have simply transferred existing and tested fundraising activities to the new medium. Very few indeed have exploited the medium with any novelty, at least up until the end of 1995. Much of the ground-breaking work in this area in the USA during 1994 was achieved by umbrella organisations working on behalf of a number of charities, rather than by individual charities (see Chapter 11).

```
THE BRITISH LIBRARY ADOPT A BOOK APPEAL

Many items in the British Library's unrivalled collection of
books, manuscripts, newspapers, maps, music and stamps are
suffering from the effects of age and constant use. More mod-
ern items in particular are in a serious state of decay large-
ly because they were produced with poor quality materials.

The Adopt a Book Appeal, launched in 1987, asks for help from
the public to pay for the conservation of items from the
Library's collection. It costs about 200 pounds sterling for
the Library to give a book a full conservation: stabilising
the paper and repairing the binding. This work is all under-
taken by craftsmen and women using the traditional skills of
conservation and binding.

Sponsors giving 200 pounds sterling or more to 'Adopt a Book'
can choose the type of book they wish to adopt, and will
receive an illuminated scroll noting their name and the title
they have saved. Inside the conserved item will be a book-
plate inscribed with the adopter's name.

All others who give to the appeal will receive a card noting
the title which their donation has helped to save.

[...]
24 June 1994
```

Two of the best exponents of using World Wide Web sites to make fundraising appeals are the environmental organisations Friends of the Earth and
Greenpeace.

Friends of the Earth <http://www.foe.co.uk> launched its own WWW site in
December 1994 and from the outset it included membership and donation
information and forms. Every page on the site contains at the bottom an exhor-
tation to "Join FoE!", which is a hypertext link to the "Become a friend of the
Earth" page. This page contains a direct appeal, an encouraging "lift letter"
from Jonathan Porritt, Special Adviser to Friends of the Earth, and a form for
the new member's name, address, e-mail address, and payment method,
whether cheque, postal order, cash or credit card. FoE also offer a monthly
standing order form, a key tool of regular or committed giving. The form
includes specific suggestions for amounts that donors might wish to give,
ranging from £250 to £10; this is the commonly-used and successful method

of increasing the average donation, as used in direct mail fundraising. In fact , in many ways the FoENet membership page represents an attempt to transfer components of a direct mail appeal to the World Wide Web - appeal, lift letter, response form, plus a free (if you count e-mail as free) and instant response mechanism.

Greenpeace International offers a pledged donation form at which gives donors the option of pledging by cash, cheque or postal order. Suggested amounts of $100 and $30 are listed. Donors are asked to select the national office of the organisation to which they wish their pledge to be sent. See at <**http://www.greenpeace.org/forms/allcontr.html**> This is a sensible example of relationship fundraising in practice: most donors will wish to help their local office rather than give to the distant international body. Greenpeace is clearly keen to receive donations: the page includes a number of options to follow if for any reason the pledge is not transmitted successfully.

"Problems?

If you have problems with sending this form because your browser (such as Lynx) may not fully support all forms featured, or you get the dreaded Error 500 - whatever that means - you can also..."

Few other charities' Web pages exhibit this small but important 'personal' touch: they seem content simply to transfer their donation form in its entirety to the Web. Whilst very little can go wrong when putting a cheque in an envelope, there are occasional problems when sending a Web form, so it is reassuring to know that Greenpeace will help you through those problems.

Greenpeace International also offers a credit card donation form at <**http://www.greenpeace.org/forms/gpicontr.html**>. The text acknowledges that some donors might prefer not to send their credit card details in this way, but at least it provides the option to do so. This seems to have paid off. International Fundraising & Marketing Director Daryl Upsall reported in September 1995 that the site was generating hundreds of donations. Significantly, after Greenpeace had begun to request that donors send donations in US dollars rather than their local currency, which was incurring bank charges, the average donation increased substantially.

The Shakespeare Globe Trust's WWW site <**http://www.globe.jhc.net/**> is another fine example of a professional and well-thought out approach to using the Internet. As well as a "virtual tour" of the reconstructed Globe Theatre, visitors are given examples of how much a particular donation will buy, with the opportunity to sponsor rebuilding items such as £500 for a theatre seat with your name on it, £300 for a flagstone, and £100 for a bushel of thatch. Secure credit card donations are encouraged, using the encryption software Netgain.

The Globe Theatre's site is interesting because it offers a comprehensive fundraising package; as well as using the secure credit card donation facility, visitors can use the non-secure donation form, find out about the need for corporate support, get involved in schools fundraising, or join a Friends scheme. The site also offers a free gift for visitors to leave with, always a good draw on a Web page. A screensaver of quotations from Shakespeare's sonnets and plays is available for download. Sensibly, when it is installed and run the user is reminded that it came from the Globe Theatre and that donations are welcomed.

Local and community group appeals on the Web

Organisational size and reputation are not a prerequisite for success, if the innovative online fundraising activities of smaller charities are anything to go by. The Knockholt Carnival, held in a small village in Kent, now runs a Web site < http://www.knockholt-carnival.org.uk/>. The main page encourages people to get involved with organising fundraising events: *"forthcoming events include the Blues Evening and the Quiz Night 16th February, not forgetting the Fashion Show for ladies that are dedicated followers of fashion"*. The site is, of course, accessible throughout the world but the organisers are clearly focusing on their local community, and encouraging local people to get involved.

Other small organisations build on an existing local fundraising event by encouraging people who can not attend to pledge a donation. The Bowling Green State University Children's Miracle Network Dance Marathon <http://www.bgsu.edu/studentlife/organizations/miracle/cmn1.html> was an event held in Ohio where students danced for 32-hours to help raise money for the Children's Miracle Network. This local event was only ever likely to attract local people - those whom its organisers were trying to reach by promoting the fundraising event to the local community, in this case students at the university. However, this promotion on the Web page introduced the event to a much wider audience; visitors to the page were asked to consider a donation.

World Wide Web pages can therefore be used to address very specific and local audiences. Any further support given by visitors to the page from further afield is simply a bonus.

In Wilmington, Massachusetts, Santa Cause has set up a Web site to benefit Toys for Tots < http://www.tiac.net/users/amerins/santa.htm > . This site is also

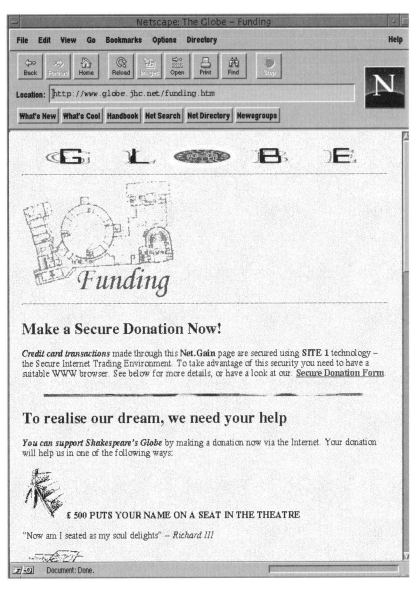

File   Edit   View   Go   Bookmarks   Options   Directory   Help

Back   Forward   Home   Reload   Images   Open   Print   Find   Stop

Location: http://www.globe.jhc.net/funding.htm

What's New   What's Cool   Handbook   Net Search   Net Directory   Newsgroups

GLOBE

Funding

Make a Secure Donation Now!

Credit card transactions made through this **Net.Gain** page are secured using **SITE 1** technology –
the Secure Internet Trading Environment. To take advantage of this security you need to have a
suitable WWW browser. See below for more details, or have a look at our **Secure Donation Form**.

To realise our dream, we need your help

You can support Shakespeare's Globe by making a donation now via the Internet. Your donation
will help us in one of the following ways:

£ 500 PUTS YOUR NAME ON A SEAT IN THE THEATRE

"Now am I seated as my soul delights" – *Richard III*

Document: Done.

To be online, or not to be...

clearly aimed at generating support from a small but core group of people, namely local citizens in conjunction with local small businesses:

"For a donation of a new toy for Toys for Tots, or at minimum $2.50 for the Wilmington Food Pantry, kids of any age (for instance: your boss, wife or neighbor) can get a personalized letter from that jolly Old Elf, signed, sealed and delivered from the North Pole.

Any resident can bring a wish letter to Santa to any of a number of "Santa Centers" in Wilmington or Tewksbury. These will be businesses dressed up for the holidays and ready to take your letter and donation. In return, Santa himself will write back".

Seeking donations is therefore not the preserve of the large national or international charities. Dozens more community, church and local groups announce their new pages on the Internet every week. Farragut High School **<http://www.nieto.com/lacrosse/knoxlax.htm>**, for example, in Knoxville, Tennessee, appeals for financial donations and gifts in kind in the form of lacrosse sticks. In fact, many of these smaller groups are so short of much-needed funds that, unlike some of the larger charities on the Internet, they incorporate fundraising appeals on their pages as soon as they are created.

In other words, small community-based nonprofits have sensibly stuck to past experience and concentrated on reaching their existing supporters and potential supporters within their local area and offering them the opportunity to get involved in fundraising for them. They have not been seduced by the global reach of the Internet and the "millions" of people "out there". The success of the Freenet system in North America, where citizens, local government and local nonprofits provide services and discuss local issues, demonstrates the value of the Internet in strengthening community ties. The original freenet, Cleveland Free-Net, is at **<telnet://freenet-in-a.cwru.edu >**.

Appeals for individuals

No group or cause is too small or unknown for its fundraiser not to test a fundraising Web page. World Wide Web appeals have even been made on behalf of a particular individual. Perhaps the most famous of these, and certainly the most apt, is the Phil Zimmermann Legal Defense Fund, whose Web pages were hosted by NetResponse **<http://www.netresponse.com>**. The Fund was set up to pay the anticipated legal costs incurred in the defence of the creator of Pretty Good Privacy ("PGP"), the popular Internet encryption program which, when exported, allegedly contravened US munitions export controls. It is ironic that the inventor of a very secure encryption program which can be

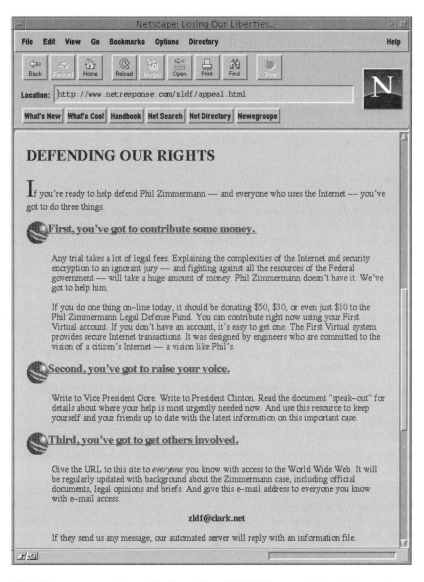

File   Edit   View   Go   Bookmarks   Options   Directory   Help

Back   Forward   Home   Reload   Images   Open   Print   Find   Stop

Location: http://www.netresponse.com/zldf/appeal.html

What's New   What's Cool   Handbook   Net Search   Net Directory   Newsgroups

DEFENDING OUR RIGHTS

If you're ready to help defend Phil Zimmermann — and everyone who uses the Internet — you've got to do three things.

First, you've got to contribute some money.

Any trial takes a lot of legal fees. Explaining the complexities of the Internet and security encryption to an ignorant jury — and fighting against all the resources of the Federal government — will take a huge amount of money. Phil Zimmermann doesn't have it. We've got to help him.

If you do one thing on-line today, it should be donating $50, $30, or even just $10 to the Phil Zimmermann Legal Defense Fund. You can contribute right now using your First Virtual account. If you don't have an account, it's easy to get one. The First Virtual system provides secure Internet transactions. It was designed by engineers who are committed to the vision of a citizen's Internet — a vision like Phil's.

Second, you've got to raise your voice.

Write to Vice President Gore. Write to President Clinton. Read the document "speak-out" for details about where your help is most urgently needed now. And use this resource to keep yourself and your friends up to date with the latest information on this important case.

Third, you've got to get others involved.

Give the URL to this site to *everyone* you know with access to the World Wide Web. It will be regularly updated with background about the Zimmermann case, including official documents, legal opinions and briefs. And give this e-mail address to everyone you know with e-mail access.

zldf@clark.net

If they send us any message, our automated server will reply with an information file.

Phil Zimmermann Legal Defense Fund WWW appeal, hosted pro bono by NetResponse, designed by Matt Dorsey.

used to send donations securely over the Internet to charities, himself ended up as the needy recipient of an Internet fundraising appeal. The appeal is now closed, because the US Justice Department has since dropped the charges.

This chapter has looked solely at using the World Wide Web to make an appeal for a straightforward donation or membership payment. While creating such a page is an essential first step, fundraisers should not stop there. There are many other ways of using the World Wide Web to raise funds (see Chapter 11) and, indeed, to make such an appeal page more effective.

Summary

- Placing a fundraising appeal and donation form on your charity's World Wide Web site is an essential first step for any fundraising activity on the Internet.

- World Wide Web appeals, like their forerunners on gopher sites, are necessarily static: to be successful they must be compelling, novel, dynamic and different.

- Do not simply state that all donations are welcome: incorporate direct mail practices such as suggesting a minimum donation.

- Offer a variety of methods of giving, from cash through postal order to travellers' cheques.

- Do offer the option to give by credit card, even if your Web page is not stored on a "secure" server: many people are happy to give by this method. Simply inform them on your page that their information will not be transmitted securely.

- The World Wide Web page can also be used to reach small, local audiences just as effectively as it can reach international audiences.

- Community, local and church groups should try to ignore the thought of 'millions of potential donors' on the Internet and instead use the Web to target their local supporters and constituents. They might number just dozens or hundreds but they are the core audience you are seeking.

9 BUILDING A FUNDRAISING WORLD WIDE WEB SITE

Fundraising is all about opportunities. Recognising opportunities, discovering opportunities, creating opportunities, developing opportunities, seizing opportunities, turning ideas into opportunities

Ken Burnett, *Relationship Fundraising*

Readers who have skipped directly to this chapter believing that this is the core of fundraising on the Internet should bear in mind the two principal themes of Chapter 2, namely:

- If you create a fundraising World Wide Web page or site without information reflecting your charity's other work, be it research, care, campaigning or advice, you will undoubtedly produce a strange first impression of your charity to any visitor.

- Creating a fundraising World Wide Web page is only one way in which a fundraiser can raise funds using the Internet. It is likely that some charities will find it far more effective to concentrate their fundraising efforts on the various applications of e-mail (see Chapter 7).

Planning

Creating a fundraising WWW page must depend on how a fundraiser has planned to integrate it within the charity's strategic plan (see Chapter 12). In short, this will reflect the goals of using the Internet, a set of realisable objectives, the tactics by which those objectives are to be met, and the application of the required resources (technical, financial, and human). It should also reflect an understanding of the likely audience that will receive the fundraising message(s) and an educated guess as to their likelihood of responding. In other words, implementing a fundraising WWW page is just like taking on any other new fundraising scheme. The same reasoning processes and criteria should be applied.

Given the widely differing types of charitable organisations, it should not be surprising that charities' fundraising WWW pages will be very varied. Some will be set up principally to seek new members or donors, others to attract corporate sponsorship, and still others to expand their trading activities. There is, therefore, no "typical" fundraising WWW page.

Domain name

If your charity does not yet have a Web site then you first need to decide what address to give it. This is becoming an important consideration in terms of marketing your online presence. If you sign up with an Internet Service Provider or use a volunteer's space on their university server you will probably end up with a long and fairly impenetrable address such as http://www.somecompany.com/~something/yourcharityname.html.

This might be acceptable during a test phase but what you really need is an address in the format http://www.yourcharityname.org which is much easier to remember, and to add to your letterhead. More importantly, once you own that name or are registered with it, the address can follow you around. If you do not like the service provided by your Internet Service Provider you can take the registered name with you to another provider but you won't have to change your letterhead and everything else that carries your Uniform Resource Locator (URL). Domain names form an important part of a charity's Internet marketing strategy.

Your domain name needs to be registered with InterNIC Registration Services. A number of companies will perform the registration for you for a price, it is usually done by your Internet Service Providers.

There is a discussion list on the practical side of using Internet domain names, including issues such as trademark registration. To subscribe send the message

SUBSCRIBE
to e-mail address: domain-name-request@mail-list.com

Creating a Web page

A World Wide Web page is actually a computer file consisting only of text. It might appear on the screen with graphics, different coloured text, formatting, and even links to sounds and video clips, but the underlying structure is text. This text is written in a language called Hypertext Markup Language (HTML) which is a standard method of presenting hypertext information. It is not a code in the sense of computer programming codes such as FORTRAN, BASIC and COBOL. It is a structured system of defining sections of text with the use of short "tags" such as <P> for new paragraph, <H1> for main heading, <B> for bold, and <LI> for items presented in a bulleted list. The good news is that perfectly presentable and functional pages can be written in HTML by a novice. With the use of the growing number of guides to HTML available in all good bookshops, the basics can be picked up in an afternoon.

There are, of course, advanced uses of HTML, in particular when it is combined with CGI (Common Gateway Interface) scripts written in the programming language Perl to allow advanced interactive options. For many charities though, basic HTML will be enough to generate the fundraising pages they want, whether it is coded by manually typing in the commands or with the use of a software package, some of which are available free of charge. As with the desktop publishing revolution, however, when owners of design software demonstrated just how lacking in formal design training they really were, the ability to use some HTML commands does not make you an accomplished Web page designer. You might choose instead to pay a professional designer.

It is probably worth pointing out that World Wide Web browsers, such as Mosaic or Netscape Navigator, do not compose HTML. They only enable you to view pages written in HTML. If you are not using a HTML editing software package you can still compose HTML using a text editor or regular word processing package. All you have to do is save the text as an ASCII file or text file. Saving the file as a Word or WordPerfect document will not work. WWW page files should also be saved with the suffix .html or .htm so that they can be identified and read by WWW browsers.

Sites with further information on HTML include:

Sandia National Laboratory HTML Reference Manual
<http://www.sandia.gov/sci_compute/html_ref.html>

Introduction to HTML
<http://www.cwru.edu/help/introHTML/toc.html>

WebTemp - a tool for creating web pages from one or more templates
<http://www.cs.curtin.edu.au/~jk/webtemp/>

HTML tips

There are plenty of books available explaining in varying degrees of detail how to create Web pages using HTML, so that subject is not touched upon here. However, there are a couple of tips on using HTML that fundraisers would do well to note.

Use the <META> tag to include keywords about the work of your charity in order to improve its relevance ranking on search engines. The more keywords you choose that match someone's search query the greater the chance that your charity will appear at the top of the list of matching sites, and so the greater the chance that your charity's site will be selected and visited. Without those keywords your charity might not appear near the top: so although it will be indexed on the search engine, in practice it will not benefit your charity much.

The <META> tag should also be used on every page to provide an out-of-date stamp such as :

<META HTTP_EQUIV="Expires" CONTENT="Friday, 26-Jan-96 09:10:40 GMT">

This should ensure that, in the case of many browsers, the most up-to-date version of your page will be viewed every time. Some browsers use a cache system which loads the most recent copy of the page from your computer's memory cache and not from the Web site itself. As the site is not itself accessed so the web server logs do not register an access, and your access statistics do not reflect the true number of hits. The above code is designed to force the browser to load the current page.

Coloured backgrounds and text can certainly enhance a Web page. However, always check that your colour schemes work. Reversed text ie white text on a dark coloured background can be difficult to read, and just as difficult to print out. This is particularly important for your online forms, many of which will be printed out by donors for faxing or posting.

Content

It is fairly widely agreed that content is king on the World Wide Web. You can have the fanciest graphics you like but people will only come back if you are offering relevant, compelling and useful information.

DETAILS ON THE CHARITY

The objects of the charity, its contact details (not just e-mail address and World Wide Web address) should be listed on the page, and arguably on all pages on the site. As with a brochure, supporters need to be informed about the need for financial support and the chances of that support being used well. Cambridge University has presented its Campaign for Cambridge brochure on its Web site
<http://www.cam.ac.uk/CambUniv/Alumni/Campaign.html>

RESPONSE DEVICE

A Web page is published to generate a response. Give visitors every opportunity you can to respond. At the very least include your e-mail address together with your name on every page. You can not assume that everyone visiting your site will do so by the "front door" of your home page. Some people will bookmark a particular page and start future visits from that page. If they have to hunt around for an e-mail address when they want to contact you they will probably not do so for long, so make it easy for them.

NAVIGATION
As some visitors will not use your home page as their first port of call, you must ensure that the structure of your site is clear. Although Web browsers allow you to return to the previous page, you should ensure that every page on your Web site contains a link back to the home page and any other general pages. Try to anticipate where visitors will wish to go. Test it: ask friends or colleagues to try out your site for ease of use.

GRAPHICS
Graphics are certainly acceptable on Web pages but they should not be over-done. Graphics can take a long time to download when viewed by a Web browser. If a visitor has to wait half a minute for one of perhaps several graphics to appear on their screen they might well cancel their visit. Therefore stick to simple and small graphics such as logos.

Graphics on Web pages are stored as .GIF or JPEG files. These are standard formats in which graphical information is compressed to take up less disk space. Most graphics packages allow you to save images in these formats. In particular you should use interlaced GIFs and ensure that they are transparent, i.e. the graphic itself blends into the background of the Web page. GIFs should also use no more than 256 colours, which helps reduce their file size and therefore ensures that they can be loaded faster.

Many of the graphics you will wish to use should already be stored in electronic format. For example your logo has probably been stored electronically by your printers to print your logo. Ask for a copy, or you will have to pay a graphics company to scan your images onto disk. If you expect to use many graphics on your Web site it might be worth investing in a scanning machine. Alternatively if you are employing a company to design and store your Web pages they should be able to cope with scanning graphics.

THE WORD "FREE"
If you want to increase the number of people visiting your site consider using the word "free". Many Web sites now use the hook of giving away something at no charge as an incentive to attract attention: <http://www.tripod.com/~tabbie/index.html>. Competitions and draws are also other ways to encourage visits and repeat visits. The Body Shop in Canada offers a free sample to visitors to its site. Charities that trade, or rather the trading subsidiaries of charities, should consider a similar approach and test its effect on the numbers visiting the site.

FURROWED BROWSERS

While Netscape remains the most popular browser you should not forget that many people visiting your site will be using different browsers and therefore your page could look quite different to them. Not all browsers support the same HTML tags, even though HTML was designed as an international standard. It is therefore worth viewing your pages using other browsers such as Mosaic, Cello, Internet Explorer, and CompuServe's SPRY. The Browser Watch site **<http://www.browserwatch.com/>** lists 57 different browsers! In particular, you cannot ignore the fact that many people will be accessing your site using a text-only browser so will be unaware of your extensive graphic design. To ensure that these visitors do not miss out on information conveyed graphically on your page you should make use of the <ALT> tag option within the <IMG SRC> tag. <ALT> gives you the chance to explain in text what the image is about. So <ALT="My charity's logo"> will yield [IMAGE = My charity's logo] on a text-only browser's view of the page.

A SIMPLE FORM

As reported in Chapter 8, many charities have begun online fundraising with a simple donation or membership form on their World Wide Web sites. Donation forms can either appear as pledge forms or as forms for credit card donations. The former require following up, usually off the Internet, whereas the latter are a direct donation. For example, the University of Saskatchewan solicits online pledges **<http://www.usask.ca/alumni/html/donation.html>** whereas KPFA Radio seeks to obtain online credit card donations **<http://www.well.com/user/kpfa/sub.html>**. Whichever you choose to offer - and it would be best to offer both - must depend on your charity's view on the issue of "security" on the Internet.

More advanced features for a fundraising Web site

The World Wide Web's flexibility is a vital strength that can be capitalised on by fundraisers. In *Relationship Fundraising* Ken Burnett asks ten marketing questions of relationship fundraisers, including *"can I think of ways to get my advertising to do 'double duty'. This is where a single effort is used to accomplish two or more different jobs. That is, can you promote organisational or brand awareness while recruiting donors, demonstrate your commitment to a particular campaign while raising funds, and so on?"* A well-constructed WWW site could achieve these and more in that it can have the "multifunctional approach" that makes a limited fundraising budget so much more productive. It can also function as another rapid-response avenue for donors' queries, doubts, criticisms and complaints, another vital service that the relationship fundraiser should offer. Burnett comments that *"fundraisers don't want dissatisfied donors out there in the cold. You want them on the inside, where you can work on them and change their minds".* E-mail links provided on a charity's WWW page can provide another avenue for such donors.

REPORTING BACK
WWW pages should provide some indication as to the success of appeals. A WWW page can be used to publish the most up-to-date information on how an appeal is progressing. In addition, annual reports can be published online as well as in paper form. Simon Frasier University, for example, has made its annual Report of Giving available online **<http://biblio.ucs.sfu.ca/development/sfuf/sfufar/sfufarhome.html>**. Initially this will not save printing costs. But over time, if you can determine whether certain donors would wish to receive the annual report in electronic form, such online publishing could help reduce printing costs.

CLUB AND FRIENDS' PAGES
The concept of adding value can be used in a number of ways by fundraisers with a World Wide Web site. Regular givers or legacy pledgers can be given access to their own "club" page via a password. This page would be unavailable to other donors and non-donors. On this page they might receive advance notice of and invitations to special events. Of course this can be taken to an extreme and some major donors at the top of the "fundraising pyramid" might perhaps be given their very own page, in recognition of their valued support. Here they could receive personalised videos or messages from the director or field staff or whatever they chose. Such pages could also be made publicly available, with the donor's permission, as a form of donor recognition. Those who leave legacies might also be recognised with a page of remembrance. This same approach can be applied to donors whether they are individuals, companies, or charitable trusts.

PRESENTATIONS TO CORPORATE OR TRUST DONORS
The World Wide Web can also be used for permanently available presentations to charitable trusts and corporate donors. By providing a URL to such a potential donor, provided that the fundraiser knows they have Internet access, an animated presentation of a project could be viewed at the grant-giving organisation's leisure, without the fundraiser necessarily being physically present. Such a page would naturally be password-protected so that only the intended prospective donor was able to view it.

Instead of World Wide Web pages, the site could also store presentation slides created in presentation software packages. A number of training presentations have been made available free of charge download by individuals and companies providing Internet training. A similar approach could be adopted for providing distance training for volunteer or regional fundraisers.

EMERGENCY AND DISASTER APPEALS

The potential of the Internet for mounting a disaster appeal has hardly been used at all. Even the most experienced and well-resourced organisation can not place a newspaper advertisement or a radio appeal in under 24 hours. Yet a WWW page could carry details and a donation form within hours (and in some cases minutes) of the disaster happening. Greenpeace placed video footage of the storming of its ship in 1995 in the Pacific by French commandos during its anti-nuclear protests on its WWW page within about an hour. Within a day or so of the Oklahoma City bombing a WWW site was established (although by individuals rather than a charity) which, as well as news and information, gave details of how to contribute to help the victims.

Following the Kobe earthquake in January 1995 a number of WWW sites were quickly created by individuals which gave information on how to make cash and material donations to help the survivors. The newsgroup alt.disasters.earthquakes, which had last sprung into action during the Los Angeles earthquake in 1994, also focused on how to send help.

News is available astonishingly quickly on the Internet. Similarly, speed is of the essence in mobilising sufficient public donations in response to a disaster. Skilled fundraisers will no doubt shortly marry the medium and the message and produce compelling disaster appeals online, as fast as the news is report-ed on conventional media. A sound knowledge of major online sources of news will help in securing hypertext links from such news organisations' Web sites to the charity's online donation form.

A prime example launching an emergency appeal rapidly on the Internet was the appeal for the victims of the Dunblane school massacre in March 1996. Within a day pledges by e-mail were being solicited, as were cheques. The option of giving over the telephone was provided, with one UK telephone number and one for those calling from abroad. A secure credit card donation form was also available within 48 hours of the Port Arthur, Tasmania, shoot-ing tragedy in May 1996: **<https://www.ausmarket.com.au/cgi/portarthur>**.

PERSONALISED DONOR PAGES

Fundraisers must strive to offer choice to donors to give them a sense of their individual worth in the eyes of the charity. On the WWW, donors could be provided with almost personalised pages if they access the charity's site with their unique membership or donor number. If the WWW page were linked to the charity's donor database (using a CGI script) the membership or donor number could be verified and, using historical information held on the donor's interests and past giving history, a personal page could be automatically con-structed in real-time. Similarly, and sooner in so far as the practice already exists, donors could be offered a personalised "newspaper" culled from their nonprofit's online documents, and this newspaper could be delivered to their desktop computer. Given the added value of such a service to donors, such a benefit could be limited to major donors or regular givers, or used as an incentive to other types of donor to upgrade donations. A free, personalised newspaper service already exists for WWW users **<http://crayon.com>**.

The same idea could be adapted to a new donor welcome package. Instead of waiting a couple of days to receive the pack through the post, a tailored welcome pack, based on the donor's expressed areas of interest, gleaned either explicitly from a brief online questionnaire or implicitly from automatic analysis of the subjects of WWW pages visited, could be mailed back automatically as soon as the online credit card donation had been received.

The above are just some of the possibilities offered to fundraisers by the World Wide Web. It is all too easy to stick to publishing a donation form on a Web page whereas, in fact, a little imagination and creativity can transform the fundraising potential of a Web site.

Further information

A free on-line tutorial for setting up Web sites designed for Lawyers, Non-Profits and Professionals is at **<http://www.collegehill.com>**.

Summary

- Plan the creation and development of your fundraising Web page as part of your overall fundraising strategy.

- Register your charity's name with the domain naming system: your own distinctive domain name is a marketing tool in itself.

- Web pages must be written in HTML. Learn the basics so that, even if you outsource the work, you can see the possibilities and issues involved

- Web page content is more important than visual appearance: plan your content to include compelling information and combine that with well-thought out navigational aids and plentiful opportunities for response

- Inspect your Web pages as read by a variety of different browsers

- Try testing different advanced uses of WWW pages such as emergency appeals, friends, club, privileged or personalised pages.

- Stand out from other Web sites: offer something different and imaginative.

10 MANAGING A FUNDRAISING INTERNET PRESENCE

"Engaging Internet members through e-mail conversations and electronic newsletters is the most widely used, and by far the most effective, form of Internet advertising".

Michael Strangelove, *Internet World*,
May 1995

Building a fundraising World Wide Web site will generate some donations. If it is to provide an effective and significant new source of revenue, the fundraiser, or more likely the fundraising manager or director, will need to manage and develop the charity's fundraising activities and presence on the Internet. At the very least, this will require a more thorough understanding of the nature of how to do business on the Internet. The lessons learned from this can then be adapted specifically to the profession of fundraising.

Marketing on the Internet

Marketing on the Internet does not consist simply of transferring existing marketing material and practices. A far more subtle model has been adopted, one which involves attracting and engaging customers and supporters with relevant and helpful information with the possibility of developing some degree of relationship with the customer: it is hoped that this relationship will produce at least one sale and preferably repeat purchases. Successful advertising on the Internet resembles far more the advertorials of print journalism than the static display advertisments of newspapers. Nevertheless, the same general marketing theories underpin Internet marketing. Ken Burnett defines marketing as *"finding out what consumers want or need and then supplying it at a profit. Research, strategy, product design, advertising, public relations, communication and even after-sales service are all part of marketing"*. Fundraisers will therefore still have to determine and display on their online appeals their "URG" (Unique Reason to Give), Burnett's translation of the marketer's USP (Unique Selling Point) to the fundraiser's lexicon.

Michael Strangelove, author of *How to Advertise on the Internet*, puts the revolutionary nature of the Internet as an advertising medium into historical perspective. First, the Internet has reversed the trend of "info-reduction", from text to sound to images, that has been the hallmark of the history of advertising, by allowing advertisers to provide more information. *"With the exception* of one-to-one personal interaction, every other medium familiar to advertisers restricted both the amount of information that could be transmitted and the degree of feedback that could be received", wrote Strangelove in *Internet World* in May 1995.

Secondly, the Internet offers advertisers a global market presence for a very small capital outlay: *"the cost of providing content on the Internet - when compared to the cost of communicating information through radio, print or television - is best described as trivial. Now $20-per-month Internet access can serve as the foundation for a global advertising campaign".*

Thirdly, the implications for small businesses, and of course small charities, are therefore immense. *"For the first time in history, the small-business world has affordable access to mass-communication and global markets through the Internet".*

The World Wide Web however is not the only method of marketing one's product or service on the Internet. *"Engaging Internet members through e-mail conversations and electronic newsletters is the most widely used, and by far the most effective, form of Internet advertising".* For this reason small businesses can compete in many ways with large businesses who have many more resources at their disposal.

The fact that *"some of the most effective cybermarketing [can be] done merely by talking with people via e-mail"* shows the levelling effect of marketing on the Internet. Tom Tabor wrote in *Internet World* (September 1995), *"Today, I think e-mail is the killer app[lication]... E-mail is still the communications tool for the overwhelming majority of the network".*

New marketing techniques and approaches are required for success in using the Internet. The straight reproduction of a printed colour brochure to a Web page, for example, fails to capitalise on the dynamic and interactive possibilities of the World Wide Web. John Hegarty, chairman of advertising agency Bartle Bogle Hegarty, argues convincingly in *The Guardian's Connect: A non-user's guide to the Internet* that advertising on the Internet involves a reversal of the traditional roles of advertiser and consumer, away from the broadcast paradigm. *"You are going to have to buy actively into the advertisement. It will have to be something you want to watch because it is interesting, not something you had to watch because it was there".*

Strangelove argues that *"a solid understanding of the nature of the Net as a new form of human communication, consumer behaviour, and virtual culture is the key to success in this revolutionary medium".* This understanding can only be gained if the company is part of the virtual community of potential and actual consumers and maintains an active presence. He concludes: *"success will go to those who enter fully into the new paradigm and transform their marketing messages into an interactive, dynamic community presence"*.

It is this level of immersion in everyday use of the Internet that will make the difference between successful online fundraisers and those who end up thinking that you can not raise funds on the Internet. Certainly, fundraisers with hands-on experience of using the Internet, whether at work or at home, will be better placed to create the innovative fundraising appeals that will succeed. However, given the amount of time required to monitor newsgroups, e-mail lists, new Internet resources and Web sites, it is also possible that specialist agencies will handle the day-to-day business of a charity's online marketing and fundraising activities, just as such agencies are contracted to carry out charities' telemarketing and advertising activities. Whether the fundraiser carries out the activities or whether the work is outsourced, the fundraiser will still need to be well-informed and experienced in using the Internet in order to brief the agency effectively and monitor its success sufficiently.

The implications for fundraisers of for-profit marketing on the Internet are clear. The Internet is a marketplace which can be entered at very low cost. It is one in which two-way relationships with customers are essential and, indeed, unavoidable. Significantly, it is a marketplace where novelty, integrity, currency and compelling content are the ingredients of success. These attributes should sound very familiar to successful fundraisers who employ them in all their other, traditional fundraising activities.

For a detailed understanding of Internet marketing issues subscribe to Glenn Fleishman's Internet Marketing list by sending a blank e-mail message to: im-sub@i-m.com or visit the list's archives at **<http://www.i-m.com>**. The list is free but the moderator suggests a voluntary once-off $25 fee. Given the high quality of the list discussion this is a price worth paying.

There is a similar moderated list focused on sales on the Internet. To subscribe to the Internet-Sales list send an e-mail with any or no message to: is-sub@mmgco.com

Neither of these lists is focused specifically on nonprofit organisations but their discussions are often equally pertinent to nonprofits.

You can also visit the Marketing Lists on the Internet website at: **<http://www.bayne.com/wolfBayne/htmarcom/mktglist.html>** and the Small Business and Effective Web Marketing site at

<http://www.wilsonweb.com/webmarket> which has articles on Web marketing, designing and promoting Web site, and WWW demographics.

The Owen Graduate School of Management at Vanderbilt University publishes research papers on marketing on the Internet. Their latest is at <http://www2000.ogsm.vanderbilt.edu/novak/new.marketing.paradigm.html>

Promoting the marketing

An essential aspect of entering this new paradigm is the practice of promoting a charity's online presence. Simply creating a Web page is not enough. "Build it and they will come," said Kevin Costner in Field of Dreams. That dream does not apply to the Internet. Existing donors have to be informed of the site's existence and potential donors have to be encouraged to visit the site. There are four different levels at which this promotion can be implemented.

REGISTERING YOUR WWW SITE

The most basic and essential step in terms of encouraging Internet users to visit your site is to register the new site with the various Internet search engines and with appropriate directories. If this is not done then it will prove very difficult for your organisation's site to be found. There are many hundreds of such search engines but it would probably not be cost effective to register with them all. Registering with somewhere between 10 and 30 of the major search engines should achieve widespread coverage.

Search engines offer different coverage of the Internet. Some directories are constructed by people, others are compiled automatically. Some dispatch "spiders" or software agents to visit World Wide Web sites, gather every word on the pages, and then add them to a central index without you registering at all.

Register at least with the search engines and directories below, although you may wish to register with more. Registering is free.

Alta Vista	http://www.altavista.digital.com
Galaxy	http://www.einet.net/
Global Online Directory	http://www.god.co.uk
InfoSeek	http://www2.infoseek.com
Internet magazine's What's New in the UK	http://www.emap.com/whatsnew
Lycos	http://www.lycos.com
OpenText	http://www.opentext.com:8080/
Webcrawler	http://webcrawler.com

What's New Too!	http://newtoo.manifest.com/WhatsNewToo/index.html
Yahoo	http://www.yahoo.com/
Yell's UK Yellow Web	http://www.yell.co.uk/

The Multimedia Marketing Group has made available their WebStep Top 100, a list of the most important 100 sites that will list a Web site at no charge <**http://www.mmgco.com/top100.html**>. It was originally an internal resource but has now been released publicly. Significantly, they also suggest an Elite 30 of the top 100, working on the interpretation of the Pareto Principle that 80% of one's business will come from 20% of clients. In other words, when registering on the Internet it is a matter of quality and not quantity. ENVision has presented a list of 150 free marketing sites, after evaluating over 700 marketing websites <**http://www.envision.net/marketing/inet/inetdata1.html**>

Registering simply involves filling in an online form at the search engine WWW site, although some accept submissions by e-mail. You will usually be asked to provide the URL of the site, the organisation operating the site, a contact e-mail address and a brief description of the site. Unfortunately some search engines can take weeks or months to include your submission, and not all of them will e-mail you to let you know that the registration has been successful. It might prove useful then to register with search engines over a period of weeks, regularly perform a search on the search engine for your charity's name and find out when it becomes available. At the same time track the number of visits to your site from Web server access logs. In this way you will gain some idea of the impact of registering with each search engine.

A number of sites claim that a single submission will automatically register your site with over 20 others. This should help save time but the practicalities are not so convincing and it might in the end be worthwhile submitting your details at each individual site. Multiple submission sites include:

The Internet Confederacy	http://www.eze.com/confederacy.html
Submit It!	http://www.submit-it.com
The PostMaster	http;//www.netcreations.com/postmaster/

There are numerous other sites that offer a free listing. You do not need to spend time getting listed on many of them. Some are there as genuine public services but others are simply ploys to attract traffic to their site, presumably so that they can claim large numbers of visitors to their clients or sponsors.

ANNOUNCING TO E-MAIL LISTS AND NEWSGROUPS

The announcement of a charity's site or of a particular major online fundraising appeal can and should be made to interested people directly and the best method of doing this is through appropriate e-mail lists and newsgroups. The key word is of course "appropriate". Spamming lists with announcements of your new site simply annoys people and generates a mailbox of criticism.

Perhaps surprisingly, it is not done to announce new sites to the various charity and fundraising discussion lists. The lists are intended as fora for discussion by nonprofit professionals, not for promoting your charity. That said, it is acceptable to respond to a query on a list about a particular type of fundraising with an informative answer which points to your Web site URL with an explanation along the lines of "have a look at how we solved that problem".

One of the most important generic announcement lists that should receive announcements of new sites is Net-Happenings, run by Gleason Sackman. To subscribe to Net-Happenings send the message:
subscribe net-happenings Firstname Lastname
to e-mail address: listserv@lists.internic.net

Newsgroups should also be used, but again it is a matter of posting to the correct place. Not surprisingly "Whonited for Charity III", the third annual Christmas fundraising drive by fans of the Dr Who TV series, was posted to rec.arts.drwho.info. The first two drives had raised £5,100 for six UK charities, and the third drive had added a seventh beneficiary. For UK charities two suitable newsgroups are uk.events, for fundraising events, online and offline, and uk.misc, a catch-all newsgroup for UK-related information.

ATTRACTING LINKS

Fundraisers must also ensure that their WWW site is linked to hypertextually by other related WWW sites. Individuals and organisations worth promoting your site to, and asking for a link to your URL include: corporate supporters; individual donors and members who have their own personal home page; local groups of supporters; suppliers; related nonprofits or charities and the Charities Aid Foundation <http://www.charitynet.org>

PAPER-BASED PROMOTIONS

Last but certainly not least, your Web site's URL should feature prominently on all material sent out of your charity's office. This should include letterheads, business cards, leaflets and brochures, annual reports, and advertisements. You could also include it on your envelope franking machine image.

Promoting a World Wide Web site is an iterative process. Fundraisers should be aware that, as new relevant sites are created, their owners should be asked to add a link to their charity's page. Most importantly, new Internet users are appearing all the time, so a system should be implemented for posting appropriate updates and announcements of any significant changes to the charity's WWW site to relevant lists and newsgroups on an ongoing basis.

Other ways to promote your site

It has already been remarked that e-mail alone can be a powerful method of communicating: in many ways it is far more effective than a World Wide Web page. Given the importance of the signature on an e-mail message (see Chapter 7), a fundraiser could try to secure organisation-wide agreement for a standard fundraising appeal to be tagged on to every individual's external e-mail message. A simple one-line message with some kind of measurable response device, such as a freephone number to call, would be all that was needed. This message could be altered monthly, or perhaps changed in response to an emergency appeal. Certainly, this is a very small promotion but it is worth testing. Finding other suitable lists or publications that will carry your information is also sensible.Chapter 13 includes information on how to search for, and identify lists on particular subjects. The Arts Deadlines list, for example, carries information on competitions, grants, scholarships etc in the arts or related areas and is sent out monthly at no charge. To subscribe to the list send the message: SUBSCRIBE DEADLINES to e-mail address: adl@rtuh.com.

The American Lung Association publicised their drawing contest on the list in March 1996, even though they did not seem to have Internet access in that they did not offer an e-mail address or a URL.

For more information on promoting your Web site you can join an e-mail list that exists to provide helpful tips on how and where to announce your Web site on the Internet. To join, send the message:
subscribe 4him-internet-tips Youremailaddress with the Subject: Subscribe
to e-mail address: hub@xc.org

You can also create .plan files to give further information on your charity's work and perhaps your current appeal. This is a text file which is accessed when someone tries to "finger" you via your e-mail address. Finger is an Internet application used to store further information on an individual.

Resourcing a fundraising Internet presence

From the above it should be clear that moving onto the Internet to develop one's fundraising is not, in practice, a cheap add-on. Not surprisingly it involves a lot of time and effort which, of course, means financial outlay. The costs of setting up a World Wide Web fundraising site, even if that includes buying a new computer and modem, will pale in comparison to the staff costs involved in planning, maintaining and developing that site. Some larger charities are already employing full-time 'Webmasters' but even these will probably not be responsible for deciding which fundraising documents should be added to the Web site and when. Certainly, organisations such as OneWorld Online remove that burden from fundraisers in that, for a set charge, they will convert all documents and graphics into HTML. Nevertheless, a fundraiser or some other member of staff will have to plan which documents to send to them for processing, and integrate that plan with other activities.

Another key resource are those staff whose responsibilities are extended to include responding to the extra enquiries generated by an Internet presence. Donors are not going to be very impressed if their e-mail queries are answered two weeks later or their credit card details are not processed until the following month, simply because there were not enough staff available to respond to the heavier workload. Inbound telephone fundraising, where charities provide a donation hotline, have provided charities with problems and challenges in dealing with various peaks and troughs of caller numbers, so experience with this should help in planning support services for an online appeal. Unlike some telephone systems which give callers an engaged tone when busy or with a call holding system which might cause some callers to give up trying to get through, e-mail messages are delivered and so require prompt response.

Introducing Internet access to a large organisation is a major undertaking. One key question is: how many staff and/or volunteers need full Internet access? If the Internet is going to be used as a research resource will all fundraisers in the team require access to it? Some organisations follow the theory that anyone who is allowed to answer a telephone should be allowed to have Internet access. Other organisations prefer to restrict the number of staff with such access. The former policy is more likely to succeed, but there will be initial errors. Perhaps the best guideline is to give e-mail access to all staff but roll out full Internet access to Usenet newsgroups and the WWW by stages.

Whoever is granted Internet access, the charity should be aware that some guidelines should be set out. The Internet can be abused just as a charity's telephone or fax could. For an example of an Internet usage policy see **<http://www.fau.edu/rinaldi/net/netpol.txt>**.

Data protection

Online fundraising brings other responsibilities. Personal information received from donors is automatically in electronic format so is covered in the UK by the Data Protection Act. Charities must ensure they are registered with the Data Protection Registrar before they handle such information. They must address the issue of security of such data, especially if it is being made available over the Internet to branch offices. The eighth Data Protection principle states that users must *"take security measures to prevent unauthorised or accidental access to, alteration, disclosure, or loss and destruction of information"*. Further information on the legal liabilities of publishing information on the Internet is available at **<http://www.poulton.com/eo-why.html>**.

Technology for technology's sake

Whoever drives a charity's fundraising presence on the Internet will determine the efficacy of the endeavour. The ad hoc arrangements that have grown from many early adopters among charities using the Internet could hinder their future development. It might seem obvious, but a charity's fundraising on the Internet should not be driven by the technology advocates. They may have valuable input but the project must be managed by a fundraiser. Some charities may place managerial responsibility for the project with the IT department. Again, this is a mistake based on confusing the medium with the skills needed to carry the message. A paper delivered by George Smith at an International Fund Raising Workshop identified technology as "the enemy of fundraising relationships". The Internet is simply a tool to assist fundraisers.

Searching for mentions of your charity

Once you have registered your URL with sufficient directories and search engines it is essential to try them out. Put yourself in the position of a would-be donor looking for your charity's site. A good search engine will return your charity's URL if the word searched for is your charity's name, but what about a more generic term? If you are an animal protection charity does your site appear when you search on "animal" and "protection"? Not everyone will search for your charity by name. If your name is not listed in the search result, but other charities are, you could lose out on enquiries and possible donations.

Once you have started using the Internet to raise funds it is surprising how your message can spread: your efforts and the work of your charity might well become the topic of conversation between people, supporters might add links to your site from their WWW pages, and other people or groups might quote from your WWW pages. Although you cannot monitor private e-mail messages you can monitor publicly-posted comments, such as those posted to e-mail lists and newsgroups.

Why might you wish to do this? With any luck most of what people will say about your charity will be positive and well-informed but some of it might not. If someone is criticising your charity in public on a Usenet discussion group their gripe will be read by dozens, hundreds and possibly thousands of people. A polite and informed official response to the newsgroup from your charity setting the record straight should allay concerns among the list and newsgroup subscribers. No reply will simply allow the complaint or criticism to fester unchallenged. We have already come across the problems caused in the 1994 Cyberspace Christmas Campaign when an individual posted incorrect instructions with regard to how to help the charities (see Chapter 11).

Your copyrighted material on your WWW page might be quoted under "fair use" provisions. But, if not, you could lose out - or information provided on your charity on other WWW sites might be out of date. A would-be donor might therefore have your old-telephone number or an out-of-date donation form, and you could lose a donation or would-be supporter.

Much of this monitoring work probably lies with the communications or external relations officer or department within a charity but there will no doubt be occasions when a reply from a fundraiser would be needed.

Monitoring for mentions of your charity on the World Wide Web and in Usenet newsgroups should also reveal whether anyone is misusing your charity's name, perhaps fraudulently. A fundraiser needs to know very quickly whether the charity's name or logo is being misused by someone to make money or in some other way that is damaging to the charity's reputation.

Searching on your charity's name might give you a surprise. It is quite likely that there is already an unofficial World Wide Web site for your charity put up by an enthusiastic volunteer. Given that many visitors to that site will assume it to be your charity's official site, you need to check that the information held is accurate. Charities with local groups might also find that their members already have local group Websites. The most practical solution for this proliferation of sites relating to your charity is to ask the owners of the other sites to add a prominent link to your official site, which will be kept up to date. The owners of the other sites should be asked not to duplicate your information, in particular addresses, telephone numbers, donation forms, and simply to provide a link to your official site which will have this information listed.

Individual supporters are already using their initiative with the Internet to raise funds for charities, in particular to promote their own fundraising events. An early example of this was a posting in December 1993 to the KIDSPHERE mailing list advertising the forthcoming Arctic Drift Stream Expedition in

February 1994. The polar travellers wished "to dedicate their expedition to fund raising on behalf of [Save the Children Fund]". Unfortunately the post did not mention how to make donations and where to send them to, a key omission that any fundraiser would have spotted. As fundraisers cannot in reality monitor and advise on every such use of the Internet by their supporters they should at least provide some guidelines on using the charity's name on the Internet and circulate this advice via existing newsletters and other publications. Newsgroups are by their nature fairly untargeted fora but some are known to have a wider and larger audience: it might, for example, be decided that, just as some charities prefer to leave contacts with national media outlets to trained staff, so supporters will be asked not to advertise their local fundraising activities in some of the major international announcement newsgroups.

Fundraising is being discussed all the time on Usenet, mostly by non-professional fundraisers. A search on "fundraising" on Dejanews in November 1995 found thousands of occurrences. Some of this homespun advice on fundraising finds its way into FAQs. For example, rec.scouting's FAQ number 7 contains a huge variety of ideas for local, volunteer-led fundraising events <http://www.cis.ohio-state.edu/hypertext/faq/usenet/scouting/7_fund-raising/faq.html>. Whilst this is an example of the manner in which expertise can be distributed, professional fundraisers should at least be aware of any such stores of advice. If they are published in the name of your charity, or if they might give the impression that they are, it will be worth nipping any incorrect or illegal advice in the bud.

If a charity still has any doubts about using the Internet to fundraise it might be worth pointing out to those who are holding the charity back that there might already be fundraising going on on the Internet in the charity's name. If anyone is going to raise money for your charity it should be yourselves!

Two case studies

Two examples of the important need to monitor the use of your charities' name on the Internet are the story of PETA and of Craig Shergold. PETA, People for the Ethical Treatment of Animals, did not register their domain name early enough. Someone else did. If you visit what you might expect to be the PETA World Wide Web site <http://www.peta.org> you will find a PETA, but this one stands for People Eating Tasty Animals, *"A resource for those who enjoy eating meat, wearing fur and leather, hunting, and the fruits of scientific research"*. Not surprisingly this is the subject of a major dispute!

In 1989 the media carried stories of a 9-year-old boy with a terminal brain tumour who wanted to achieve something before he died. Craig Shergold entered the Guinness Book of Records a year later after he received 16 million greeting cards from around the world. His tumor was successfully removed a year later. But the cards and letters continue, and the chain letter approach has now moved to the Internet. This chain letter, or one of its variations, mentions that a real US charity, the Make-A-Wish Foundation of America is involved. This is not the case but it has caused considerable problems for the organisation: staff time and resources are therefore diverted from the real work of the organisation. The Foundation has even set up a freephone number to answer the queries <**http://www.npvillage.com/wish/craig.html**>.

Summary

- Successful fundraising on the Internet will require appreciation and understanding of how the new medium works.

- Existing marketing theories still apply to the Internet but new techniques are needed: for example, you will have to promote your marketing efforts rather than let them do their work unaided.

- Promotion includes registering your site's URL at search engines and online directories, making announcements to appropriate e-mail lists and newsgroups, swapping hypertext links with other relevant sites, and listing the URL and e-mail address on every paper item issued by your office.

- Staffing is the biggest resourcing issue for running a Web site: it is much more expensive than the purchase and running costs of the IT equipment.

- How many fundraising staff in a department need Internet access? Probably not everyone, but they will all require e-mail access and training.

- Ensure that you are registered with the Data Protection Registrar if you start asking for names and addresses and other personal data via your Web page. All personal data sent via a Web page is subject to data protection law.

- Harness the enthusiasm and Internet skills that are often present within the office but do not let technophiles drive the Internet fundraising.

- Search the Internet regularly to find out if your charity is being mentioned.

11 OTHER FUNDRAISING ON THE WORLD WIDE WEB

"There are as many fundraising opportunities on-line as there are in the 'real' vs 'virtual' world. Fundraisers have never been stumped for new fundraising ideas - and it will be no different on-line"
Michael Johnston, "Fundraising on the Internet", *Professional Fundraising,* September 1995

Chapter 8 explained how charities were using their World Wide Web sites to solicit donations and recruit members. In fact there are very many other ways to raise funds using the Internet and World Wide Web in particular. Indeed almost every aspect of your current fundraising mix can be applied to the Internet. It won't necessarily be transferred literally: certain aspects will need to be translated to fit the different requirements and possibilities of the medium. For example, the long, detailed direct mail appeal that charities have found to be particularly successful might well need to be reduced in length to fit the more concise nature of documents suitable for on-screen reading.

One thing is certain: the World Wide Web is being considerably underused by charities as a fundraising tool. That is not to say that charities are not using the Web to fundraise. Some are - although far from all of those charities that have a Web presence include a fundraising appeal (see Chapter 2). However, hardly any are using the Web in the integrated manner in which it can and should be used. Many charities seem to think they are ahead of the game if they have a Web page with a donation form on it. Anecdotal evidence suggests that many of those that do this have received only modest income. Creating a Web page donation form and expecting donors to find it and use it is a very limited use of the possibilities of the World Wide Web.

Charity auctions

Online charity auctions have proved a popular use of the WWW. Perhaps inspired by the online shopping model that has guided much for-profit business activity on the Internet, charities have sensibly adapted to the Internet a trusted method of fundraising and one that is also well structured.

The Computer Museum in Boston, Massachusetts, claimed to hold the "First World Wide Web Charity Auction". It took place between 22 and 26 May 1995, and lots were on view from 16 to 21 May. The auction was held to raise funds for the Museum's educational programmes and lots included computer memorabilia, hardware and software, travel goods and artwork. The auction raised $30,000 with approximately 350 bidders and 5,000 people viewing the site during the week. The auction was so successful that biannual WWW auctions are now part of the Museum's fundraising programme.

In fact, the Computer Museum's online auction was not the first on the Internet, because Canada's first online charity auction was held in January 1995. Run by Ottawa's National Capital FreeNet, it raised $20,000. Those wishing to bid had first to register, and they then had three weeks to browse the lots. National Capital FreeNet were so happy with the result that they considered making the online auction software available to other charities for a fee, to bring in further income.

The mechanics of running the auction are up to the charity. It is certainly possible to conduct the entire process online, including the credit card donation from the successful bidder. Some charities, however, may wish to follow the practice adopted by the Montreux Counselling Centre which, when it ran an online auction, took pledges by e-mail but sent reminders to successful bidders and donors in hardcopy via the post.

Events

A charity's World Wide Web page provides another medium for advertising upcoming events such as gala fundraising occasions, benefit concerts, and sponsored events. In addition to listing events, charities could provide up-to-date figures on ticket availability for major concerts, thereby freeing fundraisers from having to answer at least some of these enquiries over the telephone.

Given the multimedia aspect of the World Wide Web, music concerts might further be advertised by providing music samples from the participating artists. Alternatively, hypertext links could be added to the artists' Web pages or to their fanclubs' pages.

Sponsored events can be promoted and an online version of the sponsor form made available for printing out and collecting sponsors' pledges, again reducing the postage and servicing overheads of the event. The Leukemia Society of America offered free marathon training through their Team in Training program on their Web site <**http://www.leukemia.org**>.

The Development Office at the University of Pennsylvania Library posted photographs of the opening of its $2 million new Business Library on its Web site <**http://www.library.upenn.edu/friends/safra.html**> within a couple of days,

File   Options   Navigate   Annotate   News   Help

Title: Red Nose–iNTERaCTIVE

URL: http://www.worldserver.pipex.com/comic.relief/intera

COMIC RELIEF

Red Nose–iNTERaCTIVE

Welcome to the section of **Red Noses in Cyberspace** that you can become a part of – Red Nose–iNTERaCTIVE.

Fund Raising Top Ten
Each one is guaranteed to be very amusing & very lucrative
These are our top ten ideas for fundraising. You can, of course, do anything you like though eating England isn't really on, but these may be some help when you're deciding. If you do your event early – try and make a short video of it. Send it in to our fundraising office as soon as you can – some of the best and funniest will be shown during the week of Red Nose Day on Channel Four's The Big Breakfast. [If you don't fancy downloading 10 sequential pages each with a 25–50K graphic, then the text–only version is for you]

The Online Red Nose Report
Here's where you can tell us all about your Red Nose fundraising event – the **Online Red Nose Report**. If you are drawing a blank about what to do for Red Nose Day then check out what like minded people are up to!

Not–A–Lottery
Run your very own Red Nose Day Office Sweepstake today!

Data transfer complete.

Back   Forward   Home   Reload   Open...   Save As...   Clone   New Window   Close Window

80

providing both news content and donor recognition.

The charity Comic Relief launched its World Wide Web site <http://www.worldserver.pipex.com/comic.relief/> in February 1995 to encourage mass participation in Red Nose Day on 17 March 1995. The site, "Red Noses in Cyberspace", included tips for the public on how to put on fundraising events.

Sponsors of charity events can publicise them free of charge on the Events Database WWW site, provided by Internet Publications Inc <http://www.ipworld.com/events/homepage.htm>. Visitors to the site can then search the database by title, location, category and date.

Corporate fundraising

Ketchum Worldwide surveyed business use of the World Wide Web in 1995 and found that more than half of the 50 largest companies in the world had established a corporate presence on the World Wide Web <http://www.ketchum.com/public_relations/public_relations.html>. Just under half of the companies surveyed published information on their philanthropic support or their involvement with public policy issues.

Given the huge number of commercial organisations which have developed World Wide Web sites in the last two years, corporate fundraising would appear to be a natural use of the World Wide Web by charities. However, although there have been a number of collaborations online between charities and for-profit organisations, it seems that in many cases the initiative was taken by the company and not the charity's fundraiser.

Fundraisers should therefore anticipate that corporate supporters might wish to extend their corporate support to the online sphere. Do you know which of your corporate supporters already have an Internet presence such as a World Wide Web site? Now is the time to find out. For smaller charities this might provide the missing link to technical skills and help in acquiring an Internet presence. All it needs is one supportive corporate donor willing to let its favoured charity benefit from its Internet experience, skills and equipment.

A number of companies have been using the World Wide Web for quite a while. The first UK consumer brand to use it, Grolsch beer, launched their site back in December 1994 <http://www.intervid.co.uk/intervid/esp/>.

Much of the corporate support that has appeared on the Internet has taken the form of companies providing free World Wide Web space and services to their partner charities. For example, MediTrust, Canada's largest mail order pharmacy, helped Easter Seals to become the "first Canadian charity on the Internet" in March 1995 by underwriting the costs associated with building and maintaining their WWW site. Right from the start the WWW site was designed to include information on how to make donations, in addition to the other information on the charity's work with children in Ontario with physical difficulties.

Offering free Web space is an astute move since a World Wide Web page costs next to nothing to create and store with the company's existing Web pages, yet the company gains good PR for its support. The charity gains valuable public exposure at no cost. However, as mentioned in Chapter 2, if the charity has no Internet access itself, then fundraisers might need to be wary of getting locked into such an arrangement. This is particularly so if the corporate donor does not agree to give priority to updating the charity's pages, moves the page's URL address, or cannot contribute staff skills required to develop a more advanced fundraising page with donation forms etc.

Other variations on the theme of corporate sponsorship have been applied to the World Wide Web. The Hermes Project, for example, a research project exploring the commercial uses of the WWW and which produces the GVU/HERMES WWW User Surveys, offered to donate $500 to each of the three most popular user-selected charities as an incentive to take part in the Third WWW User Survey and "to show appreciation to survey participants". This approach has, of course, been used with many paper surveys but it is clearly easily transferred to the WWW.

A number of companies that have established a WWW presence have implemented a corporate giving policy based on their online sales. NetBenefit <http://www.netbenefit.com>, for example, helps nonprofits raise money online. It sells music and CD-ROMs online and donates 50% of the net profit to a charitable cause selected by the purchaser. OrchidMania <http://www.orchids.org/> was set up by orchid growers to raise funds for AIDS sufferers.

Houghton Mifflin Interactive focused on the Christmas theme when they ran a campaign "to share the spirit of the holiday season with needy children". The Polar Express Share the Spirit '95 Campaign was based on a popular children's book. For every 25 e-mail messages sent to the campaign's mailbox, explaining how the sender was keeping the holiday spirit alive, Houghton Mifflin Company donated one copy of the book to a children's hospital. Between 1 November and 31 December they aimed to receive 25,000 messages, but fell just over 1,000 short of that target.

Giving a percentage of online sales to a charity is evidently a popular form of online corporate giving. Crayola's WWW page included an artwork competition with a $25,000 first prize with an announcement that the company would make a donation for every entry received to Very Special Arts, a group that helps the disabled learn via art. Bonte Sportswear Inc <http://www.catalog.com/corner/bonte> sells "environmentally friendly childrens casualwear" via its Web site and claims that each garment purchased enables the company to "save 25 sq ft of rainforest land forever". Similarly A Natural Rhythm <http://n-rhythm.com>, which sells CDs and cassettes via its Web site promise that "some proceeds go to save the Rainforests & Audubon [Society]".

Celebrity Choice Coffee sells coffee online and encourages buyers to add a donation to one of the charities listed.

Corporate giving is practised by many of the companies that produce Internet software. The developer of the SlipKnot Web shell browser software urged fellow software developers at the 1995 annual Shareware Industry Conference to follow MicroMind's lead in "donating significant portions of revenues to nonprofit and advocacy organizations". Similarly the managing director of Internet access provider Global Internet challenged the directors of other access providers to run against him in the 1996 London Marathon to raise money for United Response <**http://www.globalnet.co.uk/marathon.htm**>. He offered to pay an extra £10 for every other director that beat him.

Affinity cards that benefit charities are being marketed online. Partnerships MasterCard, a generic affinity card designed specifically for nonprofits, has been promoted since June 1995 with a World Wide Web site.

Employee participation and support for charities is another source of income which can be tapped using the Internet. Given the large number of employees who use PCs for large portions of their working days, getting a charity's message across to them via the computer desktop could well provide a cost-efficient fundraising mechanism. While employees are seldom going to be able to spend company time browsing the World Wide Web, many will be using the facilities and information resources created for them by companies' internal versions of the Internet known as "Intranets". These are private implementations of the Internet within a company or public sector organisation, within one building or perhaps linking regional and national offices. Using security measures to keep outsiders outside, Intranets use some or all of the applications of the Internet such as World Wide Web, FTP (File Transfer Protocol), gopher and newsgroup discussions to assist corporate information exchange. A large number of companies already use them and many more are following their example, with more than half of the Fortune 1000 companies in the US being expected to implement them by the end of 1996. Visa International Inc will be connecting 19,000 member banks to an Intranet in 1996.

Trials in the UK began in 1995 to determine the effectiveness of for-profit companies placing advertisements on these networks. Existing corporate supporters who have Intranets are therefore worth approaching, and asking whether they will allow a fundraising appeal area on the Intranet, or perhaps a weekly or monthly appeal on the message of the day that users see every time they start up their computers. Employers could then add their matched giving support to such donations, keeping all the activity private and internal. Of course, they could also add promotional information on their corporate and employee giving on their publicly accessible Web site.

Intranets are by nature not meant to be accessible from the outside so it is not possible to determine how much charitable support and fundraising is being carried out. Given the closely defined nature of their users, fundraising in this arena might well become a key method of employee fundraising.

Advertising

Advertising banners have appeared on many Web pages since at least early 1995. Many WWW sites are run on the basis that, whilst they do not charge for access, they derive an income from selling advertising space on their Web pages. The more people that they can demonstrate visit the page, or the more focused the type of customer that visits and, even better, buys from the site, the more the company can charge for display advertisements.

Few charities are currently deriving income from this model, yet the possibilities are certainly there. Certainly some advertisers in charities' current newsletters might be persuaded to buy an online advertisement, but so too might other organisations keen on reaching your audience. Ethical investment companies, book clubs, senior citizens' travel companies, childrens' early learning toy manufacturers - whoever might be interested in your donor profile, it is certainly worth asking them to take out an advertisement. Whilst the novelty of the Internet might appeal to some such companies, others will need convincing. This is another reason to collect data on the number of visitors to your site and any lifestyle information they might supply via a Web page form.

For a database that lists how much certain companies charge for advertising space on their Web pages, visit Publishing Alert's Online Advertising Index at <http://www.NetCreations.com/ipa/adindex/>.

Advertising can also be included in an e-mail signature, in addition to your charity's own details. A corporate supporter might be persuaded to foot the bill for your charity's Internet connection provided that every e-mail message sent from your organisation includes a one-line advertisement at the bottom along the lines of *"ABC Company <their-e-mail-address@company.com> is pleased to support XYZ charity's Internet communications"*. Such advertisements already appear on one of the nonprofit e-mail discussion lists, namely nonprofit-net run by Hubris Communications.

Trading

Publishing a catalogue online is one of the most common methods of using the WWW to generate income by for-profit companies. The considerable cost of producing and distributing a full colour catalogue of products in paper-form and the inability of any paper catalogue to reflect up-to-date stock levels and temporary price deals means that the graphical publishing qualities of the WWW were grasped early on as an additional method of selling goods, particularly mail-order goods.

Many charities, or at least their trading company subsidiaries, raise funds by selling merchandise such as clothing, stationery and publications. A number of them have begun to use their WWW sites as an additional sales outlet. Oxfam Trading, for example, includes a selection of items from its catalogue on Oxfam's OneWorld site <http://www.oneworld.org/oxfam>. The Body Shop Canada's STOP Violence Against Women's WWW site <http://www.the-body-shop.ca> includes an online catalogue where visitors can order t-shirts, flower packets and publications, and pay for them via credit card. Visitors can also obtain a discount coupon and a free sample.

Indeed, given the considerable difference in cost between producing a paper catalogue and one that exists in electronic format only, the World Wide Web might offer certain very small charities, particularly those in the South with little access to the markets of the North, their only viable method of selling goods outside their locality. One clear downside of establishing an international trading presence on the World Wide Web is, of course, setting up a fulfilment system capable of servicing all orders swiftly and efficiently. Given that orders will come in from several countries, charities with limited trading experience might not be able cope with such demands.

Nor need trading be restricted to those large charities with an established trading history. The Patriots' Trail Girl Scout Council in Boston sold a variety of their cookies via their World Wide Web page over a period of a few months and generated dozens of credit-card orders <http://www.ptgirlscouts.org>.

The World Wide Web therefore offers an additional channel for promoting and selling charity merchandise. It also in theory offers smaller charities, or charities new to trading, a cheap method of testing the water to determine whether their products are marketable. However, without enough back office systems to fulfil demand, such a test might prove troublesome.

Server statistics from World Wide Web sites should, as in other forms of online fundraising, prove valuable to the trading fundraiser. Different products can be tested against others over periods of time, products' positions on the page can be moved, special offers can be run, and the results in terms of which pages were viewed the most on which dates can be studied from the automatically-generated server logs. These amendments and tests are, of course, impossible with a paper catalogue which might be required to remain in currency for half a year or so. The country of origin of visitors to the page and/or purchasers can also be studied. A charity might wish to develop an international market but if the server logs reveal that the majority of visitors to the page are visiting from the charity's home country then the charity will clearly need to change its message or products to meet its goal.

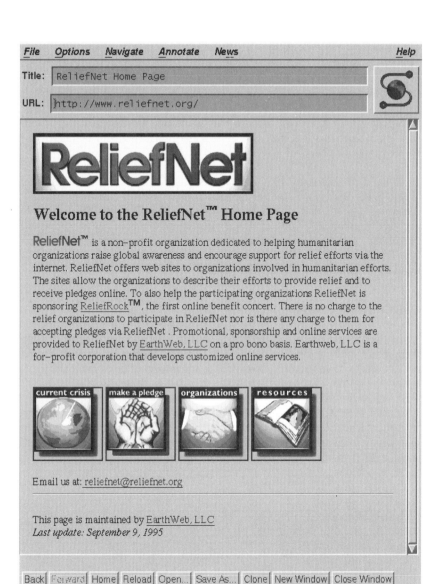

ReliefNet's WWW page

Product surveys can be added to a charity's trading page. Personal details provided by purchasers can be used to develop a profile of purchasers. The typical online buyer from a charity's catalogue will very likely be different from that of the typical buyer from the paper catalogue, and the trading fundraiser needs to know this. The fundraiser should also be collecting contact details, including e-mail addresses of both purchasers and interested visitors (with their permission) so that they can be mailed, probably via an e-mail list, to receive announcements of new products.

In addition to server statistics and product surveys, a charity trading on the World Wide Web can also offer money-off coupons as a method of tracking the use of an Internet site. Server statistics will reveal how many people accessed the coupon Web page, and your internal accounting systems will reveal how many people subsequently redeemed the coupons when purchasing. The ratio between the two figures will help give you an idea of the likelihood of generating sales from your pages.

Collaborative efforts

Many fundraising appeals on the WWW during 1994 and the first half of 1995 were made not by individual fundraisers or their charities but through a variety of collaborative ventures, usually with some form of corporate backing.

RELIEFNET AND RELIEFROCK
Launched in September 1994, ReliefNet <**http://www.reliefnet.org**> offers visitors the chance to donate to a variety of nonprofit organisations engaged in emergency relief around the world. Earthweb set it up because they were frustrated by the world community's delays in responding to major disasters, such as the genocide in Rwanda.

ReliefNet was designed from the outset both to enable electronic fundraising on behalf of nonprofit relief and development agencies and for those agencies to educate and inform the public on the need for their support. To encourage such donations, ReliefNet established "ReliefRock for Rwanda" on its WWW site, the world's first online benefit concert. Visitors were encouraged to download music samples from international artists such as Prince, Eric Clapton and Neil Young and then make online charitable pledges to one of the charter participants in ReliefNet, such as Oxfam America, CARE, YMCA and International Medical Corps. Pledges are sent directly to the chosen nonprofit, whose staff then arrange collection from the donor, whether by mail or telephone. In this way, no funds or credit card details are transferred via the ReliefNet site so the system avoids the possible dangers of sending unencrypted credit card details over the Internet.

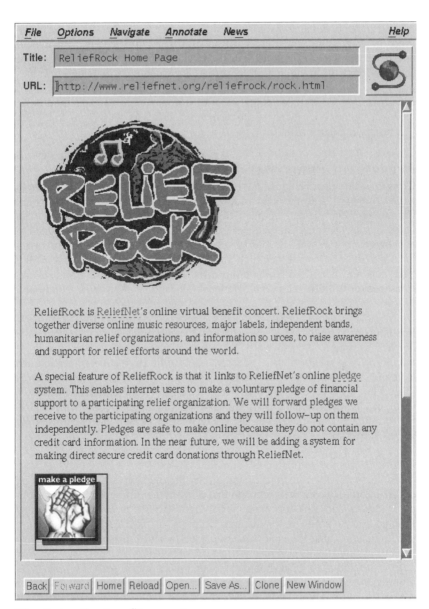

Title: ReliefRock Home Page

URL: http://www.reliefnet.org/reliefrock/rock.html

ReliefRock is ReliefNet's online virtual benefit concert. ReliefRock brings together diverse online music resources, major labels, independent bands, humanitarian relief organizations, and information so urces, to raise awareness and support for relief efforts around the world.

A special feature of ReliefRock is that it links to ReliefNet's online pledge system. This enables internet users to make a voluntary pledge of financial support to a participating relief organization. We will forward pledges we receive to the participating organizations and they will follow-up on them independently. Pledges are safe to make online because they do not contain any credit card information. In the near future, we will be adding a system for making direct secure credit card donations through ReliefNet.

make a pledge

Back Forward Home Reload Open... Save As... Clone New Window

The first online benefit concert

From its launch, donations via ReliefNet were possible using the World Wide Web, gopher, telnet and e-mail, in an effort to make giving available to Internet users with varying degrees and methods of access. ReliefNet is not static and aims to highlight current crises. For example, it included information on where to donate money to help victims of the Ebola virus in 1995. ReliefNet has made it clear that it does not take a percentage of monies pledged, and nor does it charge the recipient charities for its service. In its first year it raised at least $10,000.

CYBERSPACE CHRISTMAS CAMPAIGN

Christmas and other religious festivals have often been used by fundraisers to launch appeals, and the same idea has been transferred to the Internet. Christmas 1994 yielded another collaborative fundraising campaign. The Cyberspace Christmas Campaign at the Electronic North Pole was designed to encourage corporations to "adopt" a local charity. Corporations involved included Sun Microsystems which pledged a maximum donation of $25,000. The scheme benefited four nonprofits (Second Harvest Food Bank, Chesapeake Wildlife Heritage, Harlem Educational Activities Fund, and Plugged In) in two ways.

Firstly, every time the page was accessed, the corporate sponsor for that page donated a dime to the nonprofit. Secondly, visitors were able to contribute directly to each nonprofit. The Chesapeake Wildlife Heritage organisation, for example, encouraged visitors via its Web page to volunteer their time or to make a tax-deductible contribution using the First Virtual online payment system <http://www.fv.com>, a financial services company created to enable people to buy and sell information using the Internet (which has been available since October 1994).

Unfortunately, the campaign encountered difficulties which should act as a useful lesson to charities fundraising on the Internet. Obviously not everyone on the Internet knows their way around, or even the difference between an e-mail address and a World Wide Web page address. A hoaxer encouraged Internet users to send e-mail messages to the Cyberspace Christmas Campaign site in the belief that for each e-mail message received the sponsorship organisations would donate a dime. So instead of receiving visits to the WWW pages, the site was "mail-bombed" with e-mail messages. The story was reported by the New York Times which explained that it was a hoax. Whether it was a hoax or simply a misguided attempt to get "big business" to pay up more than it planned to charity, the resultant traffic in messages caused major problems for the host computer server. One person even sent 4205 messages!

COOKIN' ON THE NET

Another major collaborative fundraising event was established in August 1995. Impact Online Inc is a nonprofit organisation that promotes citizen involvement and action through the use of modern communications technology. Using First Virtual's online payment system, Impact Online Inc solicits financial donations via its WWW page **<http://www.impactonline>**. It also runs a wanted list of items sought as in-kind donations. From August 1995 it began soliciting online donations on behalf of other nonprofit organisations via the Cookin' On The Net scheme **<http://www.cooknet.org>**.

Cookin' On The Net is *"a fundraising program designed to fund non-profit programs who get economically disabled kids access to the computer resources that will help build their futures"*. The first phase of the scheme ran from 28 August to 28 October 1995 and involved five nationally-recognised chefs each offering an appetiser recipe. Donors were encouraged to give $12 via First Virtual, with the added attraction that every donor was automatically entered into a prize draw. The project attracted a large number of commercial sponsors such as Ben & Jerry's, Novell, O'Reilly & Associates, Warner Books, Windham Hill, and WIRED magazine. These donations of time, resources and goods enabled the organisers to claim that "no group is being paid for its time and efforts". Donors could keep track of the success of the project either by viewing the daily total on the Cookin' On The Net home page or by subscribing to an e-mail list which provided weekly updates on the fundraising totals. This latter innovation, incidentally, might well become a standard offering on a charity's pages if it is committed to developing a relationship with donors.

©**Silicon Reef, Inc., and Silicon Reef, Pty, Ltd <http://www.reef.com>**

ReliefNet, the Christmas Cyberspace Campaign, and Cookin' On The Net demonstrate that fundraisers should not think purely in terms of making an appeal for their charity alone. In the case of small charities or local appeals, or those who feel their cause does not attract widespread concern, a shared presence with other charities might well attract the commercial sponsorship that an individual charity's Internet activities would not. These joint ventures will no doubt continue and spawn many variations. One such example of one of these coalitions which has received celebrity support can be found at the Doonesbury Electronic Town Hall <**http://www.doonesbury.com/main.html**>. Here cartoonist Garry Trudeau is encouraging readers of his Doonesbury cartoon strip to get involved with four charities, the Center for Plant Conservation, the Coalition for the Homeless, Human Rights Watch and Trees for the Future. All profits from Doonesbury merchandise, which is also promoted on the Web site, are split between the four charities.

Ongoing research (see Chapter 13) in the form of monitoring relevant newsgroups and e-mail lists should give interested charities advanced notice of such schemes. ReliefNet, for example, was announced (and its pros and cons hotly debated!) on Usnonprofit-l.

Fundraisers on fundraising on the Internet

On a number of occasions during 1994 and 1995 fundraisers on the various e-mail discussion lists have debated the possibilities of fundraising on the Internet. Apart from the general acceptance that mass cold e-mail appeals are to be avoided at all costs, a number of interesting suggestions have been made.

James Bechtel, Assistant Director - Financial Development at YMCA of the USA - listed five aspects of fundraising which could be conducted using the Internet: research, marketing, cultivation, "the ask", recording/acknowledgement. He felt "the ask" or the direct appeal was currently the least applicable aspect of fundraising to the Internet, although "as the net speeds up I picture a direct mail piece that leads into a video of your program, with links to other information, and a second video of someone you know asking for a donation".

Adam Corson-Finnerty, Director of Development and External Affairs at the University of Pennsylvania Library, saw five different methods of using the WWW to raise funds. His "Library Fundraising on the Web" article was based on the experience of a small team who had designed a "Friends and Benefactors" homepage for their library. In order of priority he suggested using the WWW for donor recognition on the grounds that *"the Web allows you to recognise your donors in spectacular ways... With the Web you can create a homepage with the donor's picture... We have been calling this "elec-*

tronic plaquing"... It can be a very powerful motivator for new donors, as well as a strong re-enforcer for current donors". Such donor recognition is used at Fitchburg State University **<http://www.fsc.edu/devel.htm>.**

Secondly, Corson-Finnerty recommended using the WWW for major gift fundraising: *"bring a major prospect to your library and show them how others have been recognized on the Web".* He added however that *"People don't "give" to the Web, people give to people".*

Thirdly, the WWW could be used for *"building your friends ' group... For starters, put up your Friends' Calendar and a description of what the Friends is all about. Then add an interactive form whereby visitors can join the Friends then-and-there... Put your Friends newsletter on-line. Publicize Friends' gifts and recent acquisitions".*

Fourthly, the WWW could be used for *"Education about library goals and gift opportunities: start putting up the "picture" of where your library is heading... How about a "virtual tour" of the library?... The possibilities are only limited by the number of fundraising projects you care to manage".*

Fifthly, Corson-Finnerty suggests fundraising itself, but recommends not devoting too much energy to it. *"Record companies may sell CDs over the net, but it seems unlikely that you'll sell a $250,000 renovation to someone cruising your site. The Web homepage will be an aid to your efforts - much as a well-written brochure might be - but it won't do your work for you!"*
An e-mail discussion list was created in 1995 specifically for nonprofit staff to discuss how charities can and should use the Internet. Set up by Hubris Communications, nonprofit-1 has included a number of discussions about how best to fundraise on the Internet. Subscription details are listed in Chapter 4.

Summary

- The World Wide Web is being considerably underused by charities.

- Online auctions have been attempted with some success: the structure of the event seems to lend itself well to the World Wide Web.

- Events can be promoted online, tickets sold, and sponsorship forms distributed cheaply.

- Local volunteers can receive information on local fundraising events, and access guidance on how to run a fundraising event

- Companies are on the Internet in large numbers and many are happy to extend their corporate support to the online world too, with sponsorship, secondment and donations. Employee participation can be encouraged in the growing number of companies that use Intranets.

- Advertisements on Web pages can be bought and sold.

- Charity trading can be conducted over the World Wide Web, with graphics of products presented. Some sites are now offering money-off coupons to help track usage of the Web site.

- Many of the early fundraising events on the Internet were collaborative ventures, such as ReliefNet, the Cyberspace Christmas Campaign, and Cookin' on the Net. Such joint ventures might appeal to a band of small community groups eager to share costs between them.

- The fundraising e-mail discussion lists are fertile ground for discussions on the wide range of possible online fundraising activities.

12 INTEGRATING THE INTERNET WITH A FUNDRAISING PROGRAMME

A successful online fundraising appeal, whether by e-mail or on the World Wide Web, will work only if it reflects the current fundraising activities of the charity. Such online appeals will not be simple reproductions of printed fundraising appeals but will be versions of them, edited to fit the medium. In short, a charity's fundraising activities on the Internet must be planned and integrated with its traditional fundraising activities. There is no point in having one part of the fundraising mix emphasised simply because the other fundraisers were not interested in promoting their fundraising activities on the Internet. That will simply provide a lop-sided fundraising page. Similarly the site must be kept up to date: allowing the Christmas appeal to remain on the site until June the next year will not produce a good impression to visitors to the Web site. The Internet is different but, at the same time, it is only another tool and should therefore be subject to the same strategic planning processes as the other components of the fundraising mix.

More than a donation form

Charities that stop at transferring their donation or membership form to the

World Wide Web are creating a dull site and are almost certainly turning down the possibility of receiving other types of donation. If you are engaged in some form of fundraising it should be reflected on your World Wide Web site or in your e-mail signature.

The Friends of the Earth Web site, for example, reflects a wide range of fundraising activities and suggests that there are many different ways in which to get involved. The site is used to promote FoE's Bike to the Future event, the nonprofit's annual sponsored bike ride. It also includes details of the FoE trading catalogue. The catalogue is also linked to the Green Guide to Christmas WWW campaign page which listed a 24-hour telephone number for visitors wishing to receive a copy of the catalogue. The whole WWW site itself was made possible by a corporate donation from Sun Microsystems (UK) Ltd in the form of a SPARCserver 20 computer. In return they are credited with a banner advertisement on the page, which is itself a link to the company's homepage. This integrated approach is essential to cater for the wide variety of visitors to the site. The company director, for example, who visits the page might not be enthusiastic about becoming an individual member but the corporate sponsorship banner on every page might remind them of the company's corporate giving budget.

Statistics

Fundraisers thrive on information, or at least timely, accurate and relevant information. Information on individual donors, their interests, concerns, dislikes, past giving history and, of course, contact details, is essential to the efficient and effective generation of income. The management of information in electronic form using databases is now the norm in charities. Such electronic data is gathered, manipulated, interpreted and applied to enhance a charity's fundraising potential. Fundraising on the Internet can be integrated comfortably with such systems, not least because the information it generates on donors and visitors is automatically in electronic format.

It is all very well to create a WWW site, but how can you quantify its success? The number and total of donations received via e-mail, and via forms printed out from the Web site and then mailed or faxed, will be key. But fundraisers need accurate figures for the number of times that the site and its constituent pages have been visited, otherwise the endeavour cannot properly be evaluated. It might, for example, be the case that you are very successfully attracting thousands of people to your donation page but something is then causing people to hold back. Alternatively, you might be attracting very few visitors to the page but the conversion rate to actual donors is very high.

Fortunately for fundraisers, WWW servers automatically keep a log of the number of accesses to individual pages stored on the server. This data is ideal for fundraisers because it provides quantitative information on the popularity of the pages. Furthermore, new software packages such as Wusage **<http://www.boutell.com/wusage>** allow for increasingly sophisticated levels of information to be derived from the data, such as the domain type of the visitor. The logs can reveal whether a visitor was registered with a commercial company (.com or .co), another nonprofit organisation (.org), or from an educational institution (.edu or .ac). However, inferences about the visitor drawn from their domain names are not as accurate as was originally expected (a visitor from a .com need not be visiting the page on behalf of the company but (mis)using the company's Internet account for personal use). They do still yield valuable visitor information, however. For example, if most of your visitors are from other charities then you are not succeeding in reaching your intended audience of individuals. If most of your visitors are from overseas you might have to publish information explaining how they might wish to support you. You could, for example, let US donors know if they can make a tax-deductible donation to your organisation.

Web access statistics will be vital for internal use in managing the contacts with Internet users and adapting the site's content to meet their requirement, but outside organisations will find them useful as well. Potential advertisers will need to know how many visits your pages are attracting, just as they need to know the sales figures for a magazine.

Unfortunately, the validity of Web access statistics is widely questioned. For example, 1,000 accesses (or "hits") do not always mean 1,000 accesses by distinct individuals: they could in theory refer to 1,000 visits by the same person. Access statistics based on Web server logs are not by any means comparable to, for example, the accurate and detailed response statistics that fundraisers are used to from direct mail campaigns.

Efforts are being made to create software products to produce reliable figures which are useful both within an organisation and also enable accurate comparisons with other sites. For example, the US Audit Bureau of Circulations, the largest circulation-auditing organisation in the world, began a trial project in October 1995 to audit and verify the number of accesses to the Web pages of four newspapers and periodicals. Such independent verification of Web sites will prove a valuable boost to the development of online advertising.

It will also aid fundraisers and their media buyers in selecting the most appropriate online site or publication to advertise in. Fundraisers can not only sell advertising space on their charity's Web site but they can, of course, buy advertising space on other sites. Heavily-used search engines and major corporate sites are particularly popular sites for placing an advertisement, and some of these sites are already offering free advertising to nonprofits. Amnesty International, for example, had a banner advertisement for a while on the Webcrawler site in October 1995. Banner advertising, in which a small graphic advertisement, often a hypertext link to a company's site, appears on a WWW page, has already proved successful for the five companies that advertised on the popular directory site Yahoo! All five advertisers renewed their contracts after the three-month trial period; ten more companies, including American Express, Bank of America, Samsung and Citibank signed up.

Online questionnaires

Fundraisers already run regular questionnaires to donors, members, supporters or trading catalogue purchasers to find out more about them in order to meet their requirements more closely. This usually takes the form of a questionnaire, sometimes distributed to new donors, perhaps on the first anniversary of their gift. A charity's World Wide Web site can be used to fulfil the same function.

A fundraiser will be far more interested in the profile of the actual donors and visitors that are attracted to the charity's WWW page, rather than the profile of the forty or sixty million Internet users around the world. Web server statistics will only reveal so much, so it is essential to ask information directly from donors or visitors to the site. The value of domain name analysis has already been questioned: fundraisers should be more interested in the comments of individuals visiting their sites than in making assumptions about them from the Internet Service Provider they use.

A questionnaire form on a Web page can be used to acquire any kind of personal information that the visitor chooses to provide. (Fundraisers should be aware that since this information is automatically sent and stored electronically this activity will be covered by Data Protection legislation.) The offer of an incentive such as a regular prize draw for all respondents can be used in an attempt to increase the response rate.

Certainly results from these questionnaires will be skewed due to self-selection by the respondents but the information will surely be useful throughout the charity. Names and addresses (both postal and e-mail) can be captured automatically and integrated, with permission, with the rest of the charity's mailing activities. Respondents expressing interest in a particular theme of the nonprofit's work can then be sent regular updates on that area, thereby drawing them towards the organisation and developing a relationship with them.

This relationship can be conducted via e-mail mailing list, or by regular mail: testing will determine which is more effective.

It is clear that there is a growing audience of existing and potential donors who use the Internet and who can be contacted through the medium. As further studies of world and national user trends are conducted, fundraisers will be able to hone their appeals on the Internet in the same way that they segment donor databases to tailor their message. Micromarketing within a relationship fundraising model will undoubtedly become the key method of successful fundraising on the Internet.

Relationship fundraising on the Internet

The relationship fundraising model can be applied successfully to the Internet but is evident on very few charity fundraising sites. It is possible that donors recruited through the Web sites which offer nothing more than a donation form are being successfully integrated into the relationship model off-line and go on to form a lasting relationship with the charity. But it would seem that the relationship potential of the Internet itself is not being utilised.

Relationship fundraising is, in Burnett's words, *"an approach to the marketing of a cause which centres not around raising money but on developing to its full the unique and special relationship that exists between a charity and its supporter"*. Burnett pointed out, before the exponential growth in Internet activity, that *"tomorrow's donors, raised on increasingly sophisticated media, will also expect quality communication (no more bleak, grey, badly designed publications) and will expect to be communicated with via the most modern media, such as fax and video"*. "And the Internet" could reasonably be added in a future edition.

Burnett lists three principal methods of approaching prospective donors - by mail, telephone and in person. The Internet offers a fourth. The WWW is a new marketing paradigm, as has already been argued, in that it includes aspects of all three methods of approach. A charity WWW page can contain the text of the current direct mail appeal, a relevant sound or video-clip, and an e-mail link direct to a fundraiser or donor support officer, or perhaps even a direct video-link using software such as CUSeeMe's video conferencing, or via one of the Internet telephone systems now available.

Research is a key component of all fundraising activities, particularly within a relationship fundraising model where understanding your donor is a key factor. It follows, therefore, that researching donors and supporters recruited via a charity's Internet presence must be integrated into the fundraising strategy.

The Internet is an interactive medium. Internet users expect to be able to respond to the information they access. For this reason the Internet is an excellent medium for the relationship fundraiser. The use of a simple WWW form or <mailto> HTML tag can enable a fundraiser to receive near-instant feedback from donors or prospects visiting the charity's WWW site. To many donors this will be the equivalent to the valued telephone helpline that relationship fundraisers have offered for a number of years, allowing a direct personal contact between fundraiser and donor.

In particular, the Internet allows almost real-time testing for fundraising appeals. Constant testing is an essential aspect of direct mail fundraising: one theme is tested against another by sending it to different segments of a donor-base. In this way the fundraiser gains a knowledge of which types of appeal are more likely to succeed. However, this information usually takes a number of weeks if not months to accumulate, as some donors can take a while to mail in their donation form. A charity's WWW page, on the other hand, can be constructed in such a way that the donor or prospect has a choice of perhaps three types of project. Each one might be represented with a thumbnail graphic or photo. Each image would be linked to further information on that particular project and a uniquely identified donation form which could only be accessed from that particular route. In other words, there would be three almost identical donation forms, one for each project theme. Analysis of WWW access logs will determine which of the three projects proved of most interest to donors, and how many were moved to visit the donation form. The fundraiser could then compare the number of visits to this form with the number of donations actually received from each donation page, each of which would be uniquely identified, perhaps with a hidden HTML field.

This information can be viewed effectively as soon as the WWW page is published. Poorly performing WWW pages can then be altered or substituted to improve response, and at a fraction of the cost in terms of the time and money involved in redesigning a direct mail pack. The fundraiser can therefore strive at all times to make the charity's WWW pages relevant to donors and prospective donors. Needless to say, the profile of an online donor need not necessarily match that of the charity's more traditional donor. Iterative testing is the only way to find out: "... test, test and test again. Never give up testing", as Burnett advises.

Bad relationship fundraising on the Internet is very easy. Just as "most direct mail is mediocre and is met with indifference" so too might online charity appeals begin to look similar and unfocused: "'junk' of course isn't unique to direct mail". Fundraisers must strive to avoid the online version of 'junk mail' if the medium is not to gain a bad reputation among donors. After all, Burnett points out that "junk fundraising [via direct mail]... is causing damage to all fundraising organisations... It is even threatening the continuation of direct mail fundraising as we know it". One solution would be for fundraisers themselves, or their professional bodies, to ensure that their code of ethics and acceptable practice covers the new possibilities offered by online fundraising.

Training

Fundraisers who are new to integrating the Internet with their fundraising can be assisted and supported by the various training courses now available. There are a number of training courses for US fundraisers in using the Internet, some of which have been running since early 1995. By early 1996 *The Chronicle of Philanthropy*'s e-mail announcement of events was listing at least one Internet training session per issue, many of them directed at fundraisers. UK charity staff can now attend Internet training courses, including some specifically on fundraising on the Internet.

Outsourcing

Given the skills needed to fundraise on the Internet effectively, another area that will no doubt grow is the level of outsourcing that develops in Internet fundraising. Should fundraisers conduct fundraising on the Internet in-house or should such activities be passed to an established Internet marketing agency, just as media buying and direct mail are in many larger charities? For many small charities with a sole fundraiser this might prove an attractive solution. Sometimes even well-resourced charities might prefer to delegate such an activity to an outside organisation rather than invest in the training required to acquaint their fundraisers with the necessary expertise.

Integrating the Internet into a charity's fundraising mix is essential. It is easy to list what needs to be done but another matter entirely to implement it successfully. Nevertheless over the next year or so, the occurrence of the URL on headed notepaper and business cards, the ability of staff to respond to donors' or supporters' e-mails on a par with other forms of communication such as fax or letters, and the incorporation of user feedback into the development of WWW pages, will reveal just how many charities see a fundraising WWW page as an end in itself or the dynamic addition to the fundraising mix that it really is.

Summary

- If you publish a World Wide Web fundraising page it must reflect the full range of fundraising activities in which you are engaged.

- Server log statistics help fundraisers gauge how effective their online appeals are in terms of online visitors.

- Server log statistics can be used to determine the most effective fundraising message and to alter it and hone it over time.

- Web questionnaires can glean other information from visitors to the site.

- Communicating with donors via the Internet is compatible with the relationship fundraising model.

- Training will form an essential part of integrating the Internet into a fundraising programme.

- As with list-buying agencies and copywriting agencies, it is possible that fundraising on the Internet will largely be outsourced to specialist agencies.

13 FINDING FUNDRAISING INFORMATION ON THE INTERNET

The Internet offers a vast collection of freely available information of practical use to fundraisers. Information is always accessible to fundraisers from many other sources, from books and directories, magazines, circulars, professional organisations, consultants, research organisations, and, of course, from other fundraisers. All these information sources, and more, have an online counterpart on the Internet, so in many ways the Internet offers a one-stop library which can serve a fundraiser's need for specific information on demand. No matter what type of fundraising one is engaged in, it is fair to say that there is information available on the Internet which will be useful. It might already exist in paper form but it is now also on the Internet.

Assessing fundraising information

Electronic information is different. A book or directory is quantifiable: it has a clearly identifiable author, publisher, date and scope. You have probably paid for it and you have a good "feel" for its quality. An online electronic version is "somewhere else" and its size, scope and accuracy is more difficult to assess at first glance. Before using electronic information a fundraiser needs to ask certain questions about it.

Who is providing the information and why?

The following provide information to fundraisers on the Internet:

- fundraising magazine and newspaper publishers
- fundraising directory publishers
- national and regional professional fundraising organisations
- fundraising service/product organisations
- fundraising consultants
- grant-making bodies
- fundraisers

They provide information for a number of reasons: for profit, mutual assistance, as a public service and for public relations. As in traditional information products and services, an organisation's name and reputation will count.

How good is the information?

In assessing the value and validity of information it is useful to apply the concepts of relevance, currency and coverage. Information presented on the Internet need not be current, and it can be difficult to find out how up to date it is. A good sign of a reliable information provider is having a date somewhere on the Web page, showing when the information was last updated.

With a hardcopy directory, it is easy to see how many pages of information it contains. With an online database that is accessed via a Web page, such coverage is much more difficult to assess. The main page might say that the provider has information on all 3,000 charitable trusts that give to the arts, but it will be very difficult for you to prove that in practice. Just how good is their primary information source? Again, with an electronic resource, the relevance of the material might not be focused enough.

Unfortunately, although there are academic methods of assessing the value of online information resources, fundraisers are going to have to stick to their own best judgement, based on previous experience with information providers and on advice from colleagues. E-mail discussion lists are a useful grapevine for finding out about and judging the value of various online resources.

Finding fundraising information

Before fundraisers can find the information they are looking for on the Internet, they have first to define what it is and then know where and how to look for it. The Internet is no longer the "library with the card catalogue strewn on the floor" as it was once disparagingly described. Although the information made available via the Internet is expanding considerably every day, the methods of cataloguing and searching such information are improving steadily.

It should not be forgotten, however, that one of the easiest ways to find something out is to ask an expert. Asking a person rather than conducting an online search is in many cases an essential first step which will save time and money. This is particularly so if you are trying to find out someone's e-mail address. If you have their telephone number call them and ask them what it is, rather than dial up to the Internet and search a variety of search engines. In general, the low-tech approach should also precede the high-tech approach.

The fundraising e-mail discussion lists are a valuable resource when searching for particular pieces of information. However, on some lists you might not receive assistance if list members perceive that you are being lazy in your searching. It is often good practice to list in your message the resources that you have already exhausted before consulting the list.

Searching for electronic information using an information retrieval system is a science as well as an art. The Internet search engine pages make it all look rather simple, which of course it can be. But it may take a while to get used to the discipline required to frame an effective search query. For example, do not be surprised if a search on "donors" brings up pages of information on renal transplants or how to give blood!

Different people prefer different search engines, so it is worthwhile trying out the same search query on different engines to judge which is most effective. The search engines all use different methods of indexing information and their coverage differs greatly, so even if you can find nothing on one search engine another might provide a different result.

SEARCHING FOR SOMEONE
If you are looking for an individual, or for their e-mail address, there are a number of White Page directories to search on the Internet. These include

Big Foot	http://www.bigfoot.com
Switchboard	http://www.switchboard.com
WhoWhere	http://www.whowhere.com

A selection of other services for finding people was published in the September 1995 issue of *Internet Prospector* <http://plains.uwyo.edu/~prospect/whitepg.html>

SEARCHING FOR SOMETHING

You can use WWW search engines to find references to virtually anything, such as a charity, a company, a fundraising product or service, a magazine or researched reports. New and better search engines are made available frequently. Some of the best are Alta Vista, Yahoo, Webcrawler, Lycos, Inktomi. Of these, arguably the most useful is Alta Vista, given its unparalleled coverage of Web pages and the fact that it indexes every word on every page, not just the first half dozen lines that some search engines cover.

As mentioned in Chapter 10, your charity's WWW site should be registered with the various search engines and directories that Internet users use to locate specific information. When you search for something else on one of these sites, try searching for your own charity to check it is accessible.

SEARCHING FOR A DISCUSSION LIST OR NEWSGROUP

A number of WWW sites act as directories of e-mail discussion lists. On the other hand there are some lists that are private, the equivalent of ex-directory telephone numbers, or their membership is restricted according to certain criteria. So, extensive as these listings are, they are not guaranteed to be comprehensive.

Liszt <http://www.liszt.com> contains information on about 40,000 mailing lists. It is now searchable by e-mail as well as via the World Wide Web. For information on e-mail searching, send an empty e-mail to liszter@bluemarble.net . A guide to e-mail discussion groups is available at <http://www.webcom.com/impulse/list.html>

The Usenet Info Center <http://sunsite.unc.edu/usenet-i/home.html> lists information on almost every Usenet newsgroup, including information on what the newsgroup discusses, how to find a newsgroup's FAQ, the number of messages posted to the list on a daily and monthly basis and other useful statistics. Similarly <http://alpha.acast.nova.edu/cgi-bin/news.pl> enables you to search for newsgroups relevant to a topic you are interested in.

Central searching sites

There are a number of WWW sites which allow access to a variety of search engines, all from one page, thereby saving the searcher considerable time in locating the search engines in the first place. Good examples of these central searching sites include:

Eureka	http://www.best.com/~mentorms/eureka.htm
Metacrawler	http://metacrawler.cs.washington.edu:8080/
Prime Search	http://www.delta.com/prime.com/pssearch.htm
RES-Links: The All-in-One Resource Page	http://www.cam.org/~intsci/
Search.com offers more than 250 ways to search the Net, together with a personal customisable search page	http://www.search.com

SAMPLE SEARCHABLE BUSINESS RESOURCES

Dozens more sites of use to fundraisers are reported each week. Selecting business resources from the many different types of information available, the following are just a sample of the many searchable resources available to the corporate fundraiser:

- North American fundraisers can use a telephone number look-up service for Canadian and US individuals and businesses at <http://wyp.net>. The site will also allow a free Web page for individuals and businesses.

- Area codes for any city in the US or Canada can be searched on <http://www.555-1212.com/aclookup.html>

- A directory of 11 million US businesses, searchable by business name, category, city or state is at <http://www.bigbook.com>

- Details of 50,000 UK companies can be found in the UK Business Directory at <http://www.milfac.co.uk/milfac/>

- UK Business Park lists UK businesses by industry sector <http://www.zynet.co.uk/bpark/>

- The Internet Business Directory lists 20 million businesses <http://www.ibdi.com>

The easy way

As well as actively searching for information on the Internet, it is also possible to automate the task. By setting up a search profile, a search engine can periodically apply those search criteria against its database of information held on the Internet and then e-mail the results to your desktop PC. Sites that offer this type of service free of charge include:

Andersen Consulting's page lists several resources that monitor newsgroups and other information sources   http://www.ac.com/cstar/hsil/agents/

IBM's Infosage   http://www.infosage.ibm.com/
Stanford Netnews Filtering Service   http://hotpage.stanford.edu

UK Fundraising

While the fundraiser will have to do the above research as it applies to their charity and area of fundraising responsibility - unless they are willing to pay a professional searcher to do it - there are a huge number of resources that are now being made available specifically for fundraisers. In some cases these have involved organisations or individuals searching the Internet for relevant information and gathering it together in one place to save other fundraisers from doing all the legwork. That at least was how the author's site, UK Fundraising **<http://www.fundraising.co.uk>**, was developed.

Chapter 15 includes a list of Internet-based information resources of use for fundraisers. There are, of course, very many more available than those listed. Fundraisers working on particular causes and with particular audiences will find resources that are relevant to them but would be of little or no use to other fundraisers. Similarly, new resources are being reported regularly. The best way to keep track of these new resources is to join a fundraising e-mail discussion list (see Chapter 4) or to visit sites such as UK Fundraising which are regularly updated to include new resources.

Further information

For a guide to thinking critically about Web resources visit
<http://www.ucla.edu/campus/computing/bruinonline/trainers/critical.html>

The need for more online information

If, after using all these resources and searching for the information you need you find that you still can not get the information you require, you are not alone. Despite the ever-increasing quantity and quality of information of relevance to fundraisers being delivered in electronic form, there are still considerable gaps. For example, Sam Sternberg (aa002@torfree.net) argued in *The Network Observer* in October 1995 that there was not enough information provided online by US charitable grant-making foundations since *"the cutbacks in government funding mean that the public needs those funds desperately"*. UK fundraisers certainly do not enjoy anywhere near the same variety of Internet resources that their counterparts in North America do. The answer is twofold - lobby the professional fundraising and charitable bodies for these resources to be made available, or do it yourself and follow the example of those who set up discussion lists or research and publish the freely available Internet Prospector **<http://plains.uwyo.edu/~prospect>**.

Summary

- The Internet offers a huge collection of freely available information of practical use to fundraisers

- Fundraisers will require some degree of discrimination in selecting information that is relevant, current, and offers appropriate coverage.

- Asking another fundraiser is usually the best approach when looking for information: choose the low-tech approach before resorting to the high-tech search.

- The Internet offers tools to enable fundraisers to find information on individuals, on organisations and reports, on topics discussed anywhere on Usenet's newsgroups, and on other Internet resources such as e-mail lists and newsgroups on a particular theme.

- In addition to active searching, it is possible to set up an automatic and ongoing monitoring search for particular words which will deliver an e-mail to your PC informing you when and where those words have appeared on the Internet.

- The author's UK Fundraising WWW site **<http://www.fundraising.co.uk>** is the product of over two years' continuous searching of the Internet for relevant information for fundraisers, and acts as a freely-available, ready made library of online fundraising information.

- There is not enough information available for fundraisers in electronic format and online: if fundraisers find such information useful, they and their professional organisations will have to lobby for it to be provided.

14 THE FUTURE OF FUNDRAISING ON THE INTERNET

"Fundraisers are members of a profession that is one of the world's most powerful catalysts for change"

Ken Burnett, *Relationship Fundraising*

The future direction of the Internet in terms of its technological offerings is beyond the scope of this book. The possibilities created by new programming languages such as Java and such applications as Internet telephones, set against the ever-changing alliances of the corporations driving the development of the Internet, ie Microsoft, America Online, AT&T, and Netscape, contribute to a very confusing future. We know the Internet of today is very different from the Internet of just six months ago. The continued exponential growth in the number of Web sites, domain name registrations, and individuals acquiring online access means that the goal posts are moving all the time. Indeed the Internet itself will not necessarily exist in fifteen or twenty years' time, if the much-misunderstood "Information Superhighway" is ever brought in to existence.

The Internet is the latest in a series of media that can enable fundraisers to reach and communicate with donors in an increasingly personal manner. First came direct mail, then telemarketing, and now fundraising online. Each of the first two methods met with resistance within the UK nonprofit sector on the grounds that they were too much of an American phenomenon that would not work here in the UK. Over the past decade or so, however, both approaches have become widespread as a fundraising tool in the UK.

The following issues are certainly not a prescriptive guide to the future use of the Internet by fundraisers. They are ideas based not on technology-led fantasies or wishlists but on current and past practice: their listing here is simply a suggestion that they might prove significant in the future to fundraisers and are therefore worth considering now.

Security

Security of data being transmitted across the Internet is probably the biggest concern of many businesses and individuals in terms of developing online commercial transactions. The implementation of a global standard for online financial transactions will without doubt increase the value of using the Internet to fundraise.

It is good business practice to remove as many obstacles as possible to a customer's purchase. Customers expect an instant method of paying for a product: a request to post a letter or telephone to buy something ignores the dynamics of the online medium. Online payment systems therefore close the circle in which a customer visits a company's site, finds the information useful, selects a product and pays for it. From a fundraising viewpoint, donating by credit card is to be encouraged because, as Ken Burnett points out, "credit card givers tend to give up to 25 per cent more than those who just send in their cheque".

Too many people new to the Internet have fallen for the media's scare stories about the "lack of security" on the Internet, and therefore would not dream of sending unencrypted personal details such as credit card numbers. The Internet was not designed to be "secure" in all its aspects. Nor was the telephone, yet we merrily book tickets and pay for mail order items over the telephone, all within earshot of our colleagues at the office, all of whom have ready access to samples of our signature on our office correspondence. In a similar fashion we hand over our credit card to waiters and shop assistants whom we've never met who sometimes disappear with it for minutes at a time, and seldom return the carbon copies (on the hand-operated machines) which contain full details of our card plus a handy copy of our signature. Yet that level of "security" is acceptable to most people? The likelihood of a "sniffer" program intercepting your credit card details from the billions of packets of information being sent across the Internet does seem a lot more manageable in the face of the percentage of credit card theft that stems from merchants' fraud. Each organisation must discuss the issue and choose for themselves the acceptable level of risk.

It has even been suggested that the alarm over insecure credit card transmission has been willingly fanned by the credit card companies who did not foresee the massive growth in demand from Internet commerce and were not ready to take advantage of it. It is also pointed out that the on-screen alarms that announce "the information you are about to send is not secure" are produced by a company that makes money by selling secure servers.

Secure financial transactions have been possible for quite a while using a variety of methods. DigiCash and variations on eCash (electronic cash) have been running for a couple of years. Pretty Good Privacy offers such high levels of encryption that the US government initially tried to prosecute its creator for exporting a munition. Similarly, Netscape has offered secure transactions using its Secure Sockets Level (SSL) system on certain Web servers it sells, provided that they are accessed via Netscape

Navigator, the company's Web browser. (The broken key in the bottom left corner of the browser becomes whole when accessing a secure site.) This is almost a *de facto* standard in that between 70 and 80 per cent of those who use the World Wide Web access it via Navigator. A combination of SSL and "firewall" software to protect an internal computer system is now being used by the Bank of Montreal, the first major Canadian bank to support fully Visa and Mastercard purchases via the Internet.

Still, it is not quite a global standard. Nor does it allow verification of the credit card. This, after considerable delays, is now being concluded. The Secure Electronic Transaction (SET) standard now has support from Mastercard, Visa, American Express, Netscape, Microsoft and IBM.

Just as important as the need for genuine secure and authorised online payments is the implementation of micro-payments. Many charities would still welcome donations of £1 or £2, which is all some donors can afford, but if made by credit card the transaction costs start to mount up prohibitively. An online system that enabled such payments to be made with only minute transaction costs would undoubtedly stimulate the number of donations to charity. Equally, however, it might drive down the average level of donations: quantity need not be better than quality.

The concept of micro-payments or micro-donations for charities is also applicable to the sale of information to generate income. Given that many charities produce researched reports and sell them in hardcopy it might assist them to be able to sell them online. Sometimes reports might be just a page or two long and would not be worth selling for the 10p or so they cost to photocopy. If, however, a charity could charge 10p or a similar small sum online, the sum being automatically debited from the buyer's credit card, a new stream of income could be developed. The same could apply to a charity's database of information: someone wishing to use it could pay 1p per record or document retrieved. Of course, pricing models for information vary but micro-payments with negligible transaction costs might well prove another useful source of income for charities.

Tax-efficient giving

Another significant development that will boost income from Internet-based fundraising will be the introduction of digital signatures. At present it is not possible to receive tax-efficient gifts directly over the Internet, as these require a signature. The forms can be reproduced on Web sites or via e-mail autoresponders, but donors can only print them out and add their signature before faxing or posting them back to the charity.

In the USA Internal Revenue Service publications and forms are already available online in several print-ready formats - look at <http://www.irs.ustreas.gov/prod/forms_pubs/forms.html>. In 1994 16.4 million US tax forms were filed electronically. Once electronic filing becomes possible in the UK and tax-efficient forms are made available with digital signatures, one of the most important sources of long-term charitable giving will be able to be sought and received over the Internet.

Advertising

World Wide Web sites already carry "banner" advertisements. The most popular advertising model at the moment is probably the set fee. As long as you can demonstrate that you have a certain number of people accessing your pages per month then you can use that, much as a magazine sales department would, to set a certain price for an advertisement. The World Wide Web, however, offers other advertising models, such as paying in arrears a certain amount, perhaps 1p, for every time the page with the advertisement is accessed. Alternatively, there is the "click-through" model which involves the advertiser paying a probably higher fee for every time a visitor actually clicks through from the advertisement to the advertiser's site. Access figures can be taken from the Web server statistics.

Charities planning to sell space on their site need to be aware that certain companies might well prefer these models to the set fee model. At the same time, charities who raise funds using display advertisements and who wish to test such advertisements on the World Wide Web might find the latter models preferable.

Telethons

The Internet might also breathe new life into the charity telethon. Comic Relief, for example, first developed an online presence in 1995. Ken Burnett wrote that "ITV's Telethon, BBC's Children in Need, Comic Relief and so forth are... worthwhile uses of television that simply couldn't take place anywhere else. They show direct fundraising action to a huge audience made up mostly of people fundraisers could never hope to reach". Whilst there is no comparison as yet between a primetime national TV audience watching a TV programme all at the same time and those online on the Internet, the possibilities of a telethon on the Internet, perhaps over a longer space of time than one day or one evening, should not be ruled out, as the online charity auctions have shown. The Internet is already being integrated into existing telethons throughout the world, including one held in Perth, Australia, in October 1995.

Professional networking

The trend towards making contact with many more fundraisers than one would expect to communicate with by letter, telephone calls or at physical conferences will continue. Since the launch of the first fundraising e-mail list in 1989, hundreds (and now thousands) of fundraisers from around the world have grown accustomed to drawing on the combined professional expertise of their peers and counterparts.

Howard Rheingold, author of The Virtual Community, comments that *"My direct observations of online behaviour around the world over the past ten years have led me to conclude that whenever CMC [computer-mediated communication] becomes available to people anywhere, they inevitably build virtual communities with it"*. In other words, the use of electronic communications can create communities: where such communities already exist, such as a professional membership organisation of fundraisers, such electronic communications should help to further strengthen and develop them. For example, Rheingold points out that, in addition to the software agents that filter electronic information, *"we already have far more sophisticated, if informal, social contracts among groups of people that allow us to act as software agents for one another"*. This is exactly what US fundraisers do when one discovers a useful resource and shares it either on or off an e-mail list with other fundraisers. One fundraiser researched and published at no charge a 28-page paper on the comparative strengths and weaknesses of fundraising and development software. The monthly Internet Prospector on PRSPCT-L is another voluntary effort from which hundreds of fundraisers benefit.

Significantly, Rheingold remarks *"A continuing theme throughout the history of CMC is the way people adapt technologies designed for one purpose to suit their own, very different, communications needs"*. Which brings us back to the notion of adapting rather than adopting commercial practice.

The folklore of a professional organisation's members' collective experience and knowledge is seldom written down and is usually spread by word-of-mouth at conventions and meetings. Rheingold quotes Sproull and Kiesler, two social scientists who studied how people use computer-mediated communication in organisations. *"Folklore is an important part of [a profession or discipline], consisting of idiosyncratic information about how equipment really works and what tricks you have to know to get the experiment to come out right. It never appears in journal articles or manuals, and it is typically conveyed by word of mouth. With electronic communication, folklore can be more broadly accessible"*. The value of computer-mediated communication such as e-mail lists to fundraisers, so many of whom work in small organisations, away from their peers, must be clear: access to archived and searchable postings enables a collective knowledge bank to be developed and used.

Networking need not be restricted to e-mail lists. The possibilities of real-time text-based "chat" have not been investigated or used by many fundraisers, with the vast majority being content with the asynchronous nature of e-mail, i.e. you access it when you want, irrespective of when the sender sent it. This might change, however, as fundraisers look into the possibility of holding brief online chats or surgeries with donors. One other development in this area which might point to an expansion in this area was the request by a Internet consultancy in April 1996 for fundraisers to join them in a succession of Internet Relay Chat (IRC) sessions to brainstorm fundraising solutions for their charity client. After successful selection, fundraisers taking part would be paid for their participation.

If this global brainstorm is a success, it might be taken up by others within the profession, either along the same lines, or perhaps within some of the larger international organisations. There are already two internal e-mail discussion lists among fundraisers in Amnesty International, one in English and one in Spanish. IRC channels could allow general fundraising advice surgeries or they could focus on particular aspects of the profession, perhaps with invited experts to attend and field questions. All contributions to such a discussion can be automatically logged and could then be made available electronically to those unable to participate.

Remote training and distance learning

One likely use of the Internet by fundraisers is in the form of remote learning. The Internet has already been used as a training medium by Herb Wylen's Internet Works, Inc. Wylen ran an "on-line interactive workshop" entitled Grant Proposal Planning and Writing which was conducted entirely by e-mail to subscribers with e-mail access over a period of three weeks. The workshop leader presented topics daily and questions and responses were shared with subscribers, under the moderation of Mr Wylen.

Training or education by e-mail could prove a very cost-efficient method of training, particularly over a wide area. Conducted by e-mail, participating fundraisers need not all be in the same venue at the same time, saving on travel and accommodation costs. In fact, they need not be in the same time-zone. The possibilities of offering low-cost international training, whether to fundraisers from various organisations, or to those within a charity with various national or regional offices, seem attractive.

Recruitment

Online databanks of curricula vitae and resumes were recognised by many companies as a potential source of making money from the Internet. Either job-seekers paid to have their details registered and stored, or the companies doing the hiring paid to view suitable job-seekers' details.

Fundraising vacancies have been posted to various e-mail discussion lists and on various WWW sites for several years. No study has yet been made of how effective these postings are, compared with placing advertisements in the specialist fundraising or charity press. Nevertheless, it is possible that recruitment agencies might use the Internet to search for suitable candidates, either advertising on Web sites or via lists. Given the shortage of suitably experienced fundraisers in certain areas of expertise, an international search might become more common and affordable for recruitment consultants. Recruitment consultants Charity People (North), for example, have already set up a Web site to assist them in handling vacancies in the UK, Europe and the USA <http://www.users.dircon.co.uk/~charity>.

From the fundraiser's point of view, access to the Internet already provides them with unprecedented access to information about current vacancies. In addition to Charity People (North)'s Web site, UK charity recruitments are already offering contact e-mail addresses. At present, no fundraising vacancy in the UK has been advertised advising applicants visit a WWW site for more information, but this approach is already being used by UK charities for other, usually IT-related positions. The first indication that some charities are beginning to seek fundraisers with electronic information and online skills and experience came in November 1995 when the first UK fundraising job advertisements to mention using the Internet were advertised in *The Guardian* newspaper and *Third Sector* magazine.

Depending on their skills and experience of the Internet, recruitment consultants might also research particular candidates' contributions to discussion lists (many of which are archived and searchable), or to newsgroups. The Dejanews service <http://www.dejanews.com>, which searches postings sent to many Usenet newsgroups over a number of months, could be used to build up a profile of an individual's views or capabilities. Recruitment consultants might then have much more information on prospective candidates than ever before.

Privacy

Needless to say, recruitment consultants are not the only people who could use

Dejanews and similar archiving services to build up a profile of an individual's views. Fundraisers themselves could, when researching a major donor or prospect, check to see if they use the Internet and then build up information useful to their approach. Such practices will probably already contravene the existing ethical policies of the various professional fundraising bodies, not to mention data protection laws, but such bodies need to remain aware of the possible abuses of the Internet that their members might, albeit unwittingly, either perpetrate or fall victim to.

Awards

Web sites now have a category in fundraising awards ceremonies - concrete evidence that the Internet has arrived professionally. In Canada, the 1996 CCAE Prix d'Excellence has for the first time "best World Wide Web site".

Clearing Houses

Some charities are happy to share their successes on the Internet and publicise how much money they have raised, but many others are more reticent. Perhaps it is because they have been led to believe that setting up a Web page is all they have to do before the money floods in, and have been somewhat disappointed that this has not been the case. Whatever the reason, there is a dearth of reliable statistics on exactly how much money is being raised on the Internet, by and from whom. Yet this information is just the kind of detail for which many charities, large and small, are clamouring to help them decide how best to use the Internet. Accurate information need not be difficult to obtain: indeed, donors might themselves begin to ask for an online counter on fundraising pages to let them know how much a particular online appeal has raised and how much more money is required to reach the target. Cookin' On The Net <http://www.cooknet.org> set out to provide such current information.

In the absence of such developments, however, the free sharing of information and advice on the e-mail discussion lists is encouraging, and might perhaps be used as a model to develop a central clearing house of information on this and other subjects. Such a central store of freely-available case histories is not a new idea and has been proposed by others. The global accessibility of the Internet, however, might at last provide the opportunity to create such an archive. The International Fund Raising Group is already active in this area and the first fruits of their activities should be apparent by the time of the October 1996 International Fund Raising Workshop in Holland.

Information have-nots

Whilst much of the above suggests a bullish outlook on the many untried areas of fundraising on the Internet, it should not be forgotten that charities are often not in the best position to use new technology. As Leslie Regan Shade commented in her 1994 study to investigate e-mail and other internet working technologies for Ontario nonprofit and labour groups, *"although it would seem that computer networking could be a natural medium for many nonprofits, these organizations are often beset with problems that don't affect the for-profit sectors. These barriers to access include the cost of the hardware and software, cost of network connections, lack of computer or network literacy, lack of appropriate technical support, and high turn-over rate for staff and volunteers"*. Furthermore, the director of Glasnet, an Internet Service Provider in Russia, said in the *New York Times* that the Web *"is the ultimate act of intellectual colonialism. The product comes from America so we either must adapt to English or stop using it"*. Whilst these are certainly not reasons to stop using such a valuable medium for the benefit of charities and the people they serve, issues of unequal access to information and resources should not be ignored.

The Internet as Holy Grail

However the Internet develops, it will never be the sole answer to a fundraiser's communication needs as, indeed, it will never be the sole answer to an individual's communication needs. The issue of quality and reliability of information will remain crucial to fundraisers, so it is to be hoped that use by fundraisers of the Internet as a research tool will lead them to an appreciation of the benefits of commercial online information sources, such as Dialog (Knight-Ridder). Professor Clive Holtham, Bull Information Systems' professor of information management at City University, has studied the limitations of the "global superhighway" and has concluded that "the focus on a global information superhighway is diverting business attention from other more modest networks that give better added value in the short term". Not only do "more people use commercial online services than the world wide web" but also Holtham believes that this situation will continue for some time.

Fundraisers should be aware of some of the pitfalls of using the Internet. In relation to the accuracy and reliability of "free" information on the Internet, scams and confidence tricks on the Internet are not uncommon. Charities are an obvious target. The North American fundraising discussion e-mail lists have during 1995 carried a number of plausible but probably fraudulent business and service offers such as "pyramid schemes", which in Internet parlance are referred to as "make.money.quick" schemes.

There will also no doubt be people using the Internet who pose as charity fundraisers. Once this happens and is reported in the media, public confidence in supporting charities via the Internet will no doubt be dented. Fundraisers would do well to prepare for such an event and work to detect it by regularly searching the Internet for all mentions of their charity's name. At least one UK charity has found that it already "has" a WWW page. In this case the supporter had acted in good faith, but it could cause considerable problems and embarrassment if a charity were to find that its name had already been used on the Internet to seek funds unscrupulously.

Raising funds via the Internet will not supplant other more trusted forms of fundraising for many years, if at all. Fundraising on the Internet will not do away with the need for printed material such as thank you letters, appeal leaflets, donation forms, and annual reports. Even in the unlikely case of a majority of a charity's supporters developing the habit of interacting with their charity principally via electronic communications, there will still be significant numbers of donors who will expect to receive paper communications. Nevertheless, an opportunity on the scale of what the Internet represents to fundraisers in so many aspects of their work has not been presented for many years.

Grasping the opportunity

The Internet represents a significant opportunity to enhance your charity's fundraising and enhance your skills as a fundraiser. In fact, the opportunity has now been around for a couple of years. The first charities to use the Internet gained good publicity and arguably a reputation for being on the cutting edge of their work. Almost all, however, failed to spot the value of the global communications network for fundraising. So those charities, large and small, who are just getting started in this area do not have much to catch up on, and indeed they can ensure that they do not repeat the mistakes of those who lead the way. The examples mentioned in this book are the work of pioneers, learning from their mistakes as they go, but there is so very much more that can be done. There is no set way to proceed, which is part of the excitement of the opportunity, so your success in fundraising on the Internet will very much depend on your creative and entrepreneurial skills.

Charities, and the people and causes for which they work, can benefit in so many ways from developing and testing the various possibilities of fundraising on the Internet. All fundraisers have to do now is, as E.M. Forster declared, "Only connect!"

15 DIRECTORY OF INTERNET RESOURCES FOR FUNDRAISERS

The following resources for fundraisers have been selected from those published on the author's UK Fundraising World Wide Web site. The choice is designed to demonstrate the broad nature of resources available to fundraisers working in many different areas of fundraising. This directory is, therefore, far from comprehensive. Internet addresses do change from time to time and new sites appear every day, so readers are recommended to visit UK Fundraising <http://www.fundraising.co.uk> for current details.

BOOKS
The following sites contain information on the books rather than the full text of the publication.

http://www.in-net.com/resource/sprdfund.html
Fundraising Successes: Case studies of 50+ fund-raising events by Terri Horvath

NPO Webmaster - http://www.charityvillage.com/charityvillage/ad15.html
The Nonprofit Organization's Guide to Planning, Designing, Producing and Maintaining a Successful Site on the World Wide Web by Doug Jamieson

CONSULTANTS, SERVICE/PRODUCT SUPPLIERS
AM&M - http://www.demon.co.uk/ammdirect
Direct marketing and database specialists for charities, business and government agencies

British Promotional Merchandise Association - http://www.martex.co.uk/bpma/
The 750 members of the BPMA supply incentive gifts and merchandise

David Dixon Associates- http://www.dircon.co.uk/d-dixon/
Britain's leading arts fundraising agency

GENERAL FUNDRAISING INFORMATION
Exotic and unusual fundraising projects - **http://www.scbell.com/Marketing_&_Fundraising**

Fund-raising.com - http://www.fund-raising.com/nichenet/frindex.html
"The Online Fundraising Specialists" created a WWW site "to serve as a clearinghouse for fundraising information on the internet".

Philanthropy-related links- http://www.duke.edu/~ptavern/Pete.Philanthropic.html

UK Fundraising - http://www.fundraising.co.uk
Created by the author as part of an MSc dissertation on electronic sources of fundraising information, UK Fundraising was launched in April 1995. It contains information on fundraising discussion lists, events (training, conferences, seminars), professional education, examples of online fundraising, grants, magazines, specialist fundraising product and service suppliers, books, software, and current vacancies. Readers are recommended to use the site as a companion resource with this book; it offers links to sites mentioned in this text and the author is able to update the details continuously as new sites and resources become available.

GENERAL CANADIAN CHARITY INFORMATION
Charity Village - http://www.charityvillage.com/cvhome.html

GENERAL EUROPEAN CHARITY INFORMATION
German Charities Institute (Deutsches Spendeninstitut Krefeld) - http://www.dsk.de
The site offers 13,000 pages including a database with nearly 5,000 German charities, information on the German Council of Donations, vacancies in German charities, and links to other international sites.

GENERAL UK CHARITY INFORMATION

Aurelian Information Publishing Ltd - http://www.dircon.co.uk/aurelian
Publishers of Charities-On-Line and Charities-On-Line-*Express;* Charities-on-Disk; voluntary sector mailing lists and databases.

Charities Aid Foundation - http://www.charitynet.org
The site contains information on tax-efficient methods of giving, *Charity* magazine, CAF's services, and a searchable database of UK charities. CAF's Internet-related activities are developing considerably, including the hosting in February 1996 of a Corporate Philanthropy Cyberbreakfast.

CharitiesDirect - http://www.worldserver.pipex.com/hemscott/chardir/index.htm
Hemmington Scott Publishing Ltd, publishers of The Henderson Top 2000 Charities, launched CharitiesDirect in October 1995. It lists information on 5000 UK charities, listing five year income and expenditure data, professional advisers,corporate donors and their charitable expenditure. A News Service gives details of charity events, campaigns, vacancies and grant awards.

Charity Commission - http://www.open.gov.uk/charity/ccintro.htm
The Charity Commission of England and Wales

OneWorld Online - http://www.oneworld.org
One of the major nonprofit "supersites", OneWorld Online was launched in January 1995 to be "a meeting place where most of the leading UK agencies in the field have come together to share information with the widest possible audience world-wide". In addition to hosting the sites of nonprofits from around the world, OneWorld also provides extensive editorial information and resources of use to development organisations.

Voluntary Organisations Internet Server ("VOIS") - http://www.vois.org.uk
One of the UK voluntary sector's central online resources hosting a number of major charities on its supersite.

GENERAL US CHARITY INFORMATION
Charities USA - http://www.charitiesusa.com/

The Contact Center - http://www.contact.org/sample/dir.htm
The Contact Directory to Nonprofits on the Internet allows searches of nonprofits in Asia, Africa, Australia and the Pacific, Europe, Latin America, the Caribbean, the US and Canada.

Internet Nonprofit Centre - http://www.human.com/inc
Publishes information for donors.

GRANTS AND GRANT-MAKERS
ARIES - http://www.poptel.org.uk/aries/founds.html
Information on European foundations from the European Foundation Centre

The Foundation Center - http://fdncenter.org
Serving the information needs of grantseekers and grantmakers.

Council of Foundations - http://www.cof.org
The Council on Foundations, an association of foundations and corporations, serves the public good by promoting and enhancing effective and responsible philanthropy.

Global Partnership Group - http://www.gpg.co.uk
For organisations wishing to apply for European Union funds and who need partners. Registration is free.

The Grant Seeker's Guide to the Internet - by Dr Andrew J Grant and Suzy Sonenberg.
http://homepage.interramp.com/us002618/guide.htm

GrantsNet - gopher://gopher.os.dhhs.gov:70/1/Topics/grantsnet

GrantsWeb - http://infoserv.rttonet.psu.edu/gweb.htm
This site "organizes links to grants-related Internet sites and resources, including funding opportunities, grants data bases, policy developments, and professional activities". The site lists Federal and non-Federal grant programmes, grants databases and other searchable information systems, regulations and policies affecting grants, proposal development tools, and grant-related professional associations.

National Lottery Charities Board- http://www.aslib.co.uk/lottery/index.html
Lists the first awards made to UK philanthropic organisations by the Board in October 1995.

Opportunity Alert - http://nscp.fie.com/wincgi/fed/all/any/any/foa/any/keywords.exe/Menu
A free e-mail service (FEDIX) from the US Federal Information Exchange that delivers information about research and education funding. Users specify their areas of funding interest with an online form.

URL List for Grant Seekers - http://faraday.clas.virginia.edu/~ebf9q/url_list.html

INTERNET SERVICES FOR CHARITIES
Direct Connection - http://www.dircon.co.uk
Host to web sites of a number of major UK charities, offers a variety of Internet access services.

Hewitt & Johnston Consultants - http://www.io.org/~hjc/index.html
Dedicated to getting nonprofits online and investigating how they can best use the net for communications, alumni affairs, fundraising etc.

Hubris Communications - http://www.nonprofit.net
At least one UK charity has taken up Web space with Hubris.

Internet-UK's UK Charities Web Server - http://www.uk-charities.org/charity.htm
Any registered charity within the United Kingdom and Eire may offer an A4 page of information about themselves which describes their general operation and include the names of staff, job descriptions and telephone numbers, and this information will be stored free of charge.

Nonprofit Outreach Network - http://norn.org/pub/norn
Creates free web pages and/or provide free web space for nonprofits.

On-line Publishing - http://www.olp.co.uk
Clients include The Labour Party and Action on Smoking and Health

JOB-SEEKING
CharityVillage - http://www.charityvillage.com/charityvillage/career.html
Canadian nonprofit vacancies

Council for the Advancement and Support of Education - gopher://gopher.case.org/
CASE Online introduced its Job Classified service in March 1995. Jobs listed on their gopher server include fundraising positions.

NEWSPAPERS/MAGAZINES

The American Benefactor -http://www.AmericanBenefactor.com
A US national publication designed to help affluent men and women use their wealth not only to ensure personal financial security, but to improve society as well.

Charity Magazine - http://www.charitynet.org/news
Charities Aid Foundation's monthly magazine

The Chronicle of Philanthropy (USA)
To subscribe send the message:subscribe chronicle Firstname Lastname Organisation to chronicle-request@nonprofit.com
"The Newspaper of the Non-Profit World" provides a number of information services free of charge via e-mail. These include a preview of the next issue, an update on forthcoming events, conferences and workshops (divided regionally), and a list of deadlines for grant proposals. This information is available in hardcopy but is available two or three days in advance to those online (and even more for overseas subscribers), a significant advantage to those wishing to book a limited place at a seminar or to those aiming to deliver their grant proposal ahead of the rush.

The Chronicle promotes its free service as "not just a one-way pipeline. You'll be able to send messages to the editors, submit opinion articles, place advertisements, and more - all electronically". Launched on 1 November 1994 the service had about 1,100 subscribers by March 1995.

Direct Marketing News - http://www.dmnews.com
Daily update of what is new in direct marketing.

Fund$Raiser Cyberzine - http://www.fundsraiser.com

Funding Digest - http://www.fundraising.co.uk/fundraising/mags/fdigest.html
A unique fundraising information service, exclusively dedicated to the needs of UK-based voluntary organisations, charities, local authorities, and the agencies and information sources who support them. It is an up-to-the-minute guide to who has real money to give, and why. In 1995 this has meant over 550 pages and 330 articles. The Digest is designed to practically and effectively enhance your fundraising research.

The NonProfit Times - http://haven.ios.com/~nptimes/index.html
"The leading publication for nonprofit managers" has created a WWW site offering "information opportunities to learn about current events affecting nonprofit organizations in the US". Of direct interest to fundraisers are the abilities to access "original research on the top 100 charities (including financial and program performance measurements [and information on] the best cities to raise money". The publication claims that, with its information on direct mail, volunteers, special events, major gifts, planned gifts, corporate and foundation grants, "this new web site offers you the chance to travel through one of the most extensive databanks available on charitable giving and management".

Philanthropy News Digest - http://fdncenter.org/phil/philmain.html
Philanthropy News Digest is the weekly news service of the Foundation Center. The Digest abstracts philanthropy-related articles and feature stories in nationwide media.

Planned Giving Today - http://www.scn.org/ip/pgt/

Social and Charitable Cause Marketing - To subscribe: send a message with the subject sccm to michael@yrkpa.kias.com
A free monthly electronic magazine covering the issues of private industry sponsoring social and charitable causes. Also periodic pertinent e-mail news on social and charitable cause marketing.

PROFESSIONAL FUNDRAISING BODIES

Academic Library Advancement and Development Network -
http://www.library.arizona.edu/aladn/
ALADN brings together library fundraisers from academic and independent research libraries.

National Society of Fund Raising Executives
http://www.nsfre.org - The professional organisation for US fundraisers

PROSPECT RESEARCH

APRA - http://weber.u.washington.edu/~dlamb/apra/APRA.html

David Lamb's resource page for prospect researchers -
http://weber.u.washington.edu/~dlamb/research.html

Internet Prospector - http://plains.uwyo.edu/~prospect
A monthly newsletter published on PRSPCT-L listing a huge variety of online information resources for prospect researchers. Each issue is edited in turn by a team of volunteers. One of the best examples of professional fundraisers' cooperation on the Internet.

Rainforest Publications Inc - http://www.rpbooks.com
International prospect research company which runs corporate philanthropy awards and will launch Prospect Research Online service in summer 1996

RESEARCH PAPERS

AGRE, P. Ties That Bind, The Network Observer, May 1995, Vol 2 No 5

BEASLEY, A.A. E-mail Communication, prepared for Management and Organizational Behaviour, University of San Diego, 1995

Connect: A non-user's guide to the Internet, The Guardian, September 1995

DWYER, C. Web for Campaigns & Fundraising: The World Wide Web as a Campaign and Fundraising Tool [http://www.libertynet.org/~dwyer/iwcanada.html]

GVU's Third WWW User Survey [http://www.cc.gatech.edu/gvu/user_surveys/]
InterNet Info [http://www.webcom.com/walsh/stats.html]

KAMRATH, K-J. Uses of the Internet and WWW for Development
[http://weber.u.washington.edu/~dev/case96.html]. December 1995

National Opinion Polls Research Group [http://www.maires.co.uk]

REGAN SHADE, L. E-Connections: an ONIP sponsored feasibility study to investigate e-mail and other internetworking technologies for Ontario non-profit and labour groups, Ottawa, 1994

SOFTWARE

Blackbaud - http://www.blackbaud.com - Home of The Raiser's Edge

Crescendo - http://www.crescendosoft.com

The Pacific Group - http://www.pacificgroup.com/
Software products, management services and fundraising counsel for nonprofit institutions.

TAX-EFFICIENT GIVING/PLANNING

Giving to charity - tax tips - http://www.purple.co.uk/purplet/tax/chartips.html
Charity and Tax Free Giving, including information on Payroll deduction, Gift Aid, Deed of covenant, Charities Aid Foundation, and Tax tips.

Planned Giving Forum - http://www.ptec.com
A sponsored forum for planned giving professionals that enables e-mail discussion list-type postings to be made on a World Wide Web page.

TRAINING

http://www.fundraising.co.uk/fundraising/services/ccl/internet.html
Basic and advanced sessions on Fundraising on the Internet, part of Charity Consultant Ltd's *Prospecting for Gold* professional training series.

16 GLOSSARY

Acrobat - Adobe's software package for storing and displaying electronic documents so that they retain their formatting, no matter to which computer platform they are transferred. Acrobat is a standard method of storing and viewing certain documents on the Internet.

America Online (AOL) - Now the largest online service in the USA. It also has a UK version, which is still called America Online.

Anonymous FTP- A method of connecting to public FTP servers in order to access files stored on them. It is anonymous because you do not need a password, other than your e-mail address.

Application - A software program

ASCII - American Standard Code for Information Interchange.

Auto-responder - Also known as a mailbot or autobot, this is a software package that enables a standard message or file, such as a donation form, to be sent back in response to an e-mail message. The fundraiser does not have to answer the message personally because the software handles it automatically. Auto-responders are very useful for reducing the workload of sending out standard messages and forms.

Baud - A unit of signalling speed on a communications medium, such as a telephone wire, which measures the number of pulses of information per second. In practice it is acceptable to confuse it with bits per second, as in a 28.8Kbs modem, but technically they are different measurements.

Bookmark - A file that lists one or more addresses of favourite or regularly-visited Internet sites that save you from typing in the addresses again and again. Web browsers and gopher clients usually include this facility.

Boolean search - A way of searching for information, in particular words or phrases, using the operators AND, OR and NOT. World Wide Web search engines such as Alta Vista and Lycos offer Boolean search facilities for tracking down specific information.

Browser - A software program used for reading hypertext eg World Wide Web pages. Common browsers include Mosaic (and its variants), Cello, and Netscape Navigator.

Bulletin board system (BBS) - A system for exchanging information, e.g. messages, based on a single computer that is accessible to a group of other people. Access is usually gained by dialling up via a telephone line using standard communications software. Bulletin boards are not part of the Internet but are increasingly being made accessible via the Internet, ie. in terms of exchanging e-mail.

Client - Internet software programs e.g. World Wide Web browsers that run on your computer and interact with server programs on other computers.

Common Gateway Interface (CGI) - A standard method of integrating software packages such as databases and spreadsheets with World Wide Web pages. CGI scripts are written in a computer programming language called Perl. CGI scripts offer considerable interactivity on otherwise static Web pages.

CompuServe (CIS)- A US commercial online service, now available internationally, which since 1995 has offered Internet access.

Dial up - To connect with another computer or computer system using a modem, usually for limited sessions, in contrast to leased line.

Domain name system (DNS) - System for converting the numeric Internet addresses of computers and systems into more easily-recognisable domain names and vice versa e.g. 123.456.78.9 becomes myname.mycomputer.org.uk

Download - To copy or move a file from a computer on the Internet or a computer network to your computer.

E-mail - Electronic mail is a method of sending text messages and other computer files from one computer to one or many other computers via the Internet or a computer network.

Emoticon - Also known as a Smiley, a means of indicating a mood or attitude using combinations of text characters to be viewed by resting your head on your left shoulder, such as :-) which reads as a smiling/happy face. Widely used with hundreds of variations to enhance the often terse nature of e-mail messages, they are not appropriate in professional communications.

Encryption - Encoding or otherwise concealing text or files to prevent others from accessing them, often useful when sending sensitive data such as credit card details over the Internet. PGP, or Pretty Good Privacy, is a popular encryption program.

Europe Online - commercial online service.

FAQ - A list of answers to Frequently Asked Questions posted to e-mail discussion lists or Usenet newsgroups. Often a volunteer effort to collect useful information and to stop the same basic questions being asked again and again on the list or newsgroup as new members join. The best FAQ for nonprofits and charities is that of soc.org.nonprofit.

Finger - A program that provides information on Internet users. A method of finding out about a particular person or organisation with an Internet address.

FLA - Four-letter acronym, which ironically is itself a TLA or three-letter acronym. E-mail and newsgroup messages often include such abbreviations, e.g. IMHO

Flame - An angry, often abusive e-mail message, criticising or objecting to a message or comment you have sent eg to a newsgroup or e-mail discussion list. An exchange of flames, an online argument, is a flamewar. It usually achieves nothing except wasting other subscribers' time.

Freenet - A local community-based network designed to provide cheap, or even free, access to online information to citizens, usually available from libraries and community centres. Freenets have taken off in many North American cities and elsewhere.

Freeware (public domain) - Software which is given away at no charge to users. Many freeware software packages are available on the Internet. Freeware must not be confused with shareware.

FTP - File Transfer Protocol, a standard method of transferring a computer file from one computer to another via the Internet.

FYI - For Your Information, one of many TLAs (Three Letter Acronyms) that are commonly used on the Internet, particularly in e-mail messages and in Usenet newsgroups.

Gateway - A computer or computer system which acts as a bridge or link between two different computer networks, thereby enabling the exchange of files between them.

GIF - Graphics Interchange Format, a standard type of graphics file format used in incorporating images on World Wide Web pages. GIFs have the file suffix .GIF, for example, image.gif

Gopher - A method of storing information such as files on a computer in a hierarchical, structured manner. The information can then be navigated via menus.

Hit - The viewing of a World Wide Web page i.e. the accessing of the page's HTML file. Each hit is recorded automatically by the computer system on which the page is stored. Records of such hits on different pages can be interpreted to determine the number or type of visitors to a World Wide Web site. However, ten hits on a page could mean ten visitors to that page or equally it could mean one visitor accessing the page ten times.

Home page - The default World Wide Web page that is loaded when the browser is first started. It could be a personal page, a charity's main page, or the browser manufacturer's main page.

HTML - HyperText Mark-up Language is the standard Internet code in which World Wide Web pages are written. Text, graphics, sounds, video and other devices are all presented using a series of text tags, e.g. <P> signifies a paragraph break. Resultant text files are interpreted and displayed by World Wide Web browser software programs. HTML ensures that the type of computer on which the file is stored and the type of computer on which the file is viewed is effectively irrelevant. HTML offers the flexibility of storing and presenting information in hypertext.

HTTP - Hypertext Transfer Protocol is a standard method of transferring HTML documents over the Internet.

Hypertext - A way of linking information on one computer file to associated information on another. This is the method of storing and structuring information that underpins the World Wide Web. It contrasts with the rigidly structured nature of a database.

IMHO - In My Humble Opinion, another common acronym, this time, however, a four-letter acronym or FLA.

Internet Explorer - The World Wide Web browser provided by Microsoft, originally as part of its Windows 95 software

Internet Relay Chat (IRC) - An online chat system which enables you to communicate with one or more people by typing at your PC. Apart from a few seconds delay in sending and receiving messages, this is real-time chat. - the opposite to e-mail conversations which can be conducted over many hours without each person being online at the same time.

Internet Service Provider (ISP) - An organisation that provides a user or organisation with access to the Internet.

Intranet - An internal computer network within an organisation which uses Internet tools and programs for private use and restricted access only. The Intranet might allow access to the Internet to the organisation's staff but it will not allow access to unauthorised users outside the system.

ISDN - Integrated Service Digital Network provides much faster and more secure transmission of voice and computer files than that available over a standard telephone line. Consequently ISDN lines cost much more to install and use.

JAVA - A programming language that offers dynamic add-on facilities to World Wide Web pages, e.g. spreadsheets and databases, without the need to acquire those particular applications. Mini versions of these applications ("applets") are automatically downloaded as the World Wide Web page is accessed to run as the page is appears. Development of Java is heralded as changing the face of the World Wide Web.

JPEG - Joint Photographic Experts Group who produced the JPEG standard graphics file format which, like GIF, is commonly used on World Wide Web pages.

Kbps - Kilobits per second, or 1,024 bits per second. A measurement of the rate of data transfer, e.g. via a modem.

LAN - Local Area Network, a computer network usually within one organisation, which enables people to share data, e.g. via e-mail, and hardware such as printers. A LAN can be connected to another LAN or to the Internet with a gateway.

Leased line/dedicated line - A private link such as a telephone line or ISDN line that is permanently connected to the Internet. Files on a computer or network with a leased line are therefore available 24 hours a day - the opposite to a dial-up link which uses the line only for the duration of the telephone call.

Listserv - Software that runs an e-mail dis-

cussion list automatically. It is sometimes used generically of all e-mail discussion lists, irrespective of the software used to run them, e.g. Majordomo, Listproc.

Mailing list/e-mail list - A system, usually automated, that distributes e-mail messages on a specific topic to the e-mailboxes of a list of subscribers. Some lists are one-way, allowing a charity, for example, to send out regular announcements. Others are two-way and allow messages to be posted by any subscriber, thereby allowing an ongoing conversation between two or more subscribers that is viewed by all subscribers. Subscription is usually free and requires an e-mail message to be sent to the central list software program.

Majordomo - A software program that runs a mailing list.

Microsoft Network (MSN) - Microsoft's online service, renamed as the MSN Internet Online Service.

Modem - Device that converts digital data such as computer files and messages so that it can be sent across the non-digital telephone network to another computer. It then reconverts such data back into digital form that can be received and processed by a computer.

Mosaic - The first popular World Wide Web browser.

Net - An abbreviation for the Internet. Is also used to describe all online communication channels i.e. the Internet plus the commercial online networks such as CompuServe and America Online.

Netiquette - A largely unwritten set of rules of behaviour on the Internet, widely adhered to mostly because they are common sense and make life easier.

Netscape Navigator - The most popular World Wide Web browser used on the Internet, and therefore the browser you are most likely to use. Other browsers include Lynx, Mosaic and Internet Explorer.

Newsgroup - A discussion group on Usenet that focusses on a particular subject.

Newsreader - Software that enables you to access newsgroups, such as Free Agent for Windows and Newswatcher for Macintosh.

Off-line - The opposite to online, meaning not connected to the Internet.

Off-line reader - A software program that

downloads e-mail and newsgroup messages to your PC so that you can read and reply to them whilst disconnected from the Internet, thereby saving you telephone charges.

PGP - Pretty Good Privacy - encryption program for encoding e-mail messages and files.

POP - Post Office Protocol, a standard method of storing your e-mail on your Internet Service Provider's server until you connect to your ISP and the e-mail is automatically downloaded.

PoP - Point of Presence, a connection point to your Internet Service Provider, which should be in your local telephone area if you are to keep telephone costs down.

Post - Send a message to a Usenet newsgroup.

PPP - Point to Point Protocol, a standard method by which a computer can connect to the Internet using a telephone line and modem. Superceding SLIP as a method for accessing the Internet.

RTFM - Read The Flaming [your choice of expletive] Manual, a common response, particularly in Usenet newsgroups, recommending that you think harder or do some basic research yourself before you ask an obvious question that wastes other people's time.

Server - a computer that shares data with and controls its flow to other computers on a network.

Shareware - Try-before-you-buy software. Programs available, often via the Internet, free of charge evaluation for a specific time period, after which, if satisfied you should pay a registration fee, often fairly small.

Signature - A few lines of text, usually added automatically, to any e-mail message you post. It should include your name, charity, address, telephone and fax numbers, and e-mail address. E-mail users at charities should include in their signature a one-line fundraising appeal with telephone number or e-mail address for response.

SLIP - Serial Line Internet Protocol, a standard method by which a computer can connect to the Internet using a telephone line and modem. PPP is becoming more common.

Smiley - See Emoticon.

Spam - To post the same message to many and/or inappropriate newsgroups. An online version of junk mail that causes annoyance and creates an unprofessional image. It might derive from the Monty Python sketch featuring "spam, spam, spam...".

Telnet - A standard method of accessing computers in the next room or on the other side of the world from your own computer and then using them to run programs or access data.

UK Online - A commercial online service.

UNIX - A common computer operating system used on many computer networks that are linked to the Internet.

URL - Uniform Resource Locator, a standard method for describing Internet addresses. For example, http://www.fundraising.co.uk

Usenet - A huge group of computer systems that exchange discussions on thousands of topics called newsgroups. Effectively a global messaging or bulletin board system.

Uuencode - A standard method to convert binary files, e.g. word-processed documents, software programs, graphics files, to ASCII format so that they can be sent via e-mail. Without such conversion the files will not be received in any usable form. Many e-mail systems automate this process.

Veronica - A search tool that enables searches for files and directories stored on Gopher servers.

WAIS - Wide Area Information Server, a method of searching databases via the Internet.

White pages - A collection of e-mail addresses or domain names.

Whois - A program for searching for e-mail addresses.

World Wide Web/WWW/Web - A hypertext-based system for storing and retrieving information, enabling text, graphics, sound and video to be presented on screen. Other resources can be accessed via hypertext links.

Zip - A common file format for compressing computer files, usually created using the PKZIP program. Files available via the Internet are often stored in this compressed format. Such files will have the .zip suffix, e.g. filename.zip

17 BIBLIOGRAPHY

E-MAIL LISTS (CANADA AND USA)

Edupage [listproc@educom.unc.edu]
CFRNET [listserv@unc.edu]
FUNDCAN [listserv@qucdn.queensu.ca]
FUNDLIST [listproc@listproc.hcf.jhu.edu]
FUNDSVCS [majordomo@acpub.duke.edu]
GIFT-PL [listserv@indycms.iupui.edu]
GRANTS-L [listproc@sphinx.gsu.edu]
GRANTWRITER-L
[majordomo@fallingrock.com]

Internet Marketing List
INTFUND [no longer available]
KIDSPHERE [listserv@vms.cis.pitt.edu]
Net-Happenings [listserv@lists.internic.net]
NONPROFIT-NET [listproc@nonprofit.net]
PRSPCT-L [listserv@bucknell.edu]
TALK-AMPHILREV [majordomo@tab.com]
Usnonprofit-l [usnonprofit-l-
request@rain.org]

NEWSPAPERS AND MAGAZINES (UK)

Association Quest
Business Week
tCF NOW, The Charity Forum
Charity Magazine, Charities Aid Foundation
Charity Times
DONORS
The Economist
Information Age
Internet
Internet World
.net

NetUser
Online Business Today
Professional Fundraising,
Member Update Service, ICFM
Trust Monitor, DSC
The Big Issue
The Guardian Online
The Independent
Third Sector
Wired (UK)

NEWSPAPERS AND MAGAZINES (USA)

CASE Currents, CASE
The Chronicle of Philanthropy
Handsnet Weekly Digest [hn0049@hand-snet.org]
Internet-on-a-Disk [http://www.samizdat.com]
Netsurfer Digest [http://www.netsurf.com]
The Scout Report [http://rs.internic.net/scout]

SEIDMAN, R. In, Around and Online
[http://www.clark.net:80/pub/robert
/home.html]
TIDBITS [info@tidbits.com]
WEBster [http://www.6gc.com/webster.html]
Wired (USA)

BOOKS

BURNETT, K.   Relationship Fundraising, The White Lion Press Limited,
London, 1992
RHEINGOLD, H. The Virtual Community, Mandarin Paperbacks [Reed Consumer
Books], London, 1995
RODD J.   The Computers in Fundraising Research Report, Institute of
Charity Fundraising Managers, London, 1993
SPROULL, L. & KIESLER, S. Connections: New Ways of Working in the
Networked World Cambridge, Mass: MIT Press, 1991

INDEX

Also from AURELIAN

CHARITIES ON DISK

The *updating database service* for and about the voluntary sector, giving detailed contact information - address, phone, fax, charity number and subject categories for over 7000 active national charities and voluntary organisations. Information is continuously checked and revised; subscribers receive full updated data disks monthly. Disk formats to fit all mainstream database systems and loadable onto existing databases for reference/mailing needs. Instant up-to-date database details on the key organisations in the voluntary sector.

An immediate database - no research required ... With monthly updates - no need for you to revise... Categorised by subject ... easy to sort or search... Registered charity numbers for positive identification... Phone/fax and address at your fingertips... Runs on, or merges with, your in-house database system.

12 monthly disks giving regularly updated contact data for over 7000 UK national organisations. Annual Subscription: £550.00 + VAT.

MAILING LABELS AND DISKS

Contact the charities with ready-to-use self-adhesive mailing labels or single usage rental disk; selection by subject, income or geographical area.

Price per 1000 ex VAT: Labels £95.00; Disk £75.00; Selection Fee £5.00.

Internet-for-All Books

Direct Connection's *Guide to Fundraising on the Internet* is the first title in a new series of books on applied functions of the Internet and the World Wide Web. The series embraces the various topics needed for getting the greatest value from the Internet, early titles include finance and profiling across the Web. All texts are guaranteed jargon-free!

Many of the issues covered will have associated Internet training seminars. Call Aurelian Information direct to discover the training dates and venues planned for your area.

ORDERS/ENQUIRIES: AURELIAN INFORMATION LTD - UK
TEL 0181-960 7918 FAX 0171-794 8609 E-MAIL aurelian@geo2.poptel.org.uk